You Again

Dr Simon Robinson

YOU, AGAIN
© 2025 Simon Robinson
All rights reserved.

First published in 2025.

No part of this publication may be reproduced, stored in a retrieval system, or transmitted in any form or by any means—electronic, mechanical, photocopying, recording, or otherwise—without prior written permission of the copyright holder, except in the case of brief quotations embodied in critical reviews or scholarly work.

All illustrations and images are reproduced from publicly available sources identified as public domain or Creative Commons. Several images have been cropped, enhanced, or restored for clarity; such edits do not alter the underlying authorship or meaning of the original works.

Image restoration, typesetting assistance, and minor layout automation were supported by contemporary digital tools. All final editorial decisions and creative direction remain the sole work of the author.

ISBN:
Print Edition: 978-1-0684310-6-7
Ebook Edition: 978-1-0684310-7-4

Publisher of Record:
Simon Robinson
United Kingdom

Printed and distributed internationally by IngramSpark.

British Library Cataloguing-in-Publication Data:
A catalogue record for this book is available from the British Library.

For more information:
www.drsimonrobinson.com

"Welcome back, Mr. Anderson.

We missed you."

— Agent Smith
(*The Matrix Revolutions*)

Contents

List of Illustrations — xi
List of Tables — xiv
INTRODUCTION — xv

Part One: Establishing Possibility

ASK THE WISE — 2
   Philosophers and Classical Voices — 3
   Artists, Scientists, and Saints — 6
   World Religions and Traditions — 6
   Reflection — 6

Part Two: Of The Wise & Glorious

Philosophers & Classical Voices

ZHUANGZI (C. 369–286 BCE) — 4
PYTHAGORAS (C. 570–495 BCE) — 6
EMPEDOCLES (C. 494–434 BCE) — 8
PLATO (429–347 BCE) — 10
VIRGIL (70–19 BCE) — 12
PLUTARCH (C. 46–120 CE) — 14
PLOTINUS (204–270 CE) — 16
ORIGEN OF ALEXANDRIA (C. 184–253 CE) — 18
THE DRUIDS (AS REPORTED BY JULIUS CAESAR) — 20
GIORDANO BRUNO (1548–1600) — 22
GOTTHOLD EPHRAIM LESSING (1729–1781) — 24
BENJAMIN FRANKLIN (1706–1790) — 26
WILLIAM WORDSWORTH (1770–1850) — 28
ARTHUR SCHOPENHAUER (1788–1860) — 30
RALPH WALDO EMERSON (1803–1882) — 32
W.B. YEATS (1865–1939) — 34
CARL JUNG (1875–1961) — 36

Aldous Huxley (1894–1963)	38
Timothy Leary (1920–1996)	40
Ram Dass (1931–2019)	42

Artists, Writers & Musicians

George Harrison (1943–2001)	46
David Bowie (1947–2016)	48
Shirley MacLaine (b. 1934)	50

Scientists, Physicians & Psychologists

Camille Flammarion (1842–1925)	54
Thomas Edison (1847–1931)	56
Henry Ford (1863–1947)	58
W. C. Alvarez, M.D. (1884–1978)	60
Albert Schweitzer (1875–1965)	62
Ian Stevenson, M.D. (1918–2007)	64
Brian Weiss (b. 1944)	66
Jim B. Tucker M.D. (b. 1960)	68
Erlendur Haraldsson (1931–2020)	70
Satwant K. Pasricha (b. circa. 1945)	72

Religious Leaders & Mystics

Kamo no Chōmei (1153–1216)	76
Ramakrishna Paramahamsa (1836–1886)	78
Helena Blavatsky (1831–1891)	80
Annie Besant (1847–1933)	82
Sri Aurobindo (1872–1950) & The Mother (Mirra Alfassa, 1878–1973)	84
Paramahansa Yogananda (1893–1952)	86
The 14th Dalai Lama (b. 1935)	88
Mahatma Gandhi (1869–1948)	90
Winston Churchill (1874–1965)	92

World Religions & Traditions

| Hinduism: The Many Rivers of One Tradition | 96 |
| *The Soul and the Wheel of Return* | 97 |

Paths Toward Liberation	97
Living with the Sense of Return	98
Voices of Scripture	98
The Modern View and Global Influence	99
Reflection	100
Between the Rivers: From Hinduism to Buddhism	101
BUDDHISM: THE TURNING OF THE WHEEL	102
What is Reborn?	103
The Wheel of Life	103
The Law of Karma	104
Paths to Liberation	104
Mahāyāna and Vajrayāna Visions	105
Living and Dying with Awareness	105
A Universal Teaching	106
Reflection	106
JAINISM: THE RELIGION OF NON-VIOLENCE	108
Karma as Substance	109
The Journey of the Soul	109
Reflection	110
SIKHISM: A FAITH OF ONENESS	112
The Divine and the Soul	113
Karma and Grace	114
The Way of the Gurmukh	114
The Ten Gurus and the Living Word	115
Ethics and the Equality of All	115
Life, Death, and Liberation	116
A Living Faith	116
Reflection	117
KABBALAH: COVENANT & MYSTERY OF LIFE	118
The Soul in Scripture and Tradition	119
The Kabbalistic Vision	119
Life, Death, and the World to Come	120
Death and Remembrance	121
Reflection	121
CHRISTIANITY: THE PROMISE OF RESURRECTION	124

The Soul and Eternal Life	124
The Diversity of the Early Church	125
Medieval and Mystical Currents	126
Life, Death, and the Hope of Glory	126
Reflection	127
ISLAM (SUFI POETIC): THE DAY OF RETURN	128
The Nature of the Soul	129
Philosophical Interpretations	129
The Sufi Vision—Cycles of Transformation	130
Death and the Afterlife	131
Reincarnation and the Boundaries of Orthodoxy	131
Reflection	132
DAOISM: THE WAY THAT CANNOT BE SPOKEN	134
Transformation, Not Reincarnation	135
The Souls Within	135
The Search for Immortality	136
Judgment and Return	137
Mystical Rebirth	137
Life, Death, and the Flow of the Dao	138
Reflection	138
SHINTO: THE WAY OF THE KAMI	140
Life in a Living World	140
The Presence of Ancestors	141
Death and Renewal	142
Nature as Continuum	142
Reflection	143
YORUBA TRADITION: THE LIVING COSMOS	144
Destiny and the Soul (Orí)	145
Ancestral Return (Atúnwá)	145
Life, Death, and the Journey of the Soul	146
Reflection	147
AKAN TRADITION: THE BREATH OF NYAME	148
The Structure of the Person	148
Reincarnation and Ancestral Return	149
The Moral Law (Nkrabea and Sunsum)	150

Death, Funerals, and the Journey Home	150
The Wider Vision	151
Reflection	151
GRECO-ROMAN & PLATONIC TRADITIONS	154
Plato and the Education of the Soul	155
From Philosophy to Mystery	155
The Stoics and the Eternal Return	156
Neoplatonism and the Return to the One	156
The Twilight of the Ancient World	157
Reflection	157
NORSE & CELTIC TRADITIONS	160
The Norse: Wyrd and Return	160
Ancestral Rebirth	161
The Afterlife of Heroes	161
The Celts: The Ever-Living Ones	162
The World of the Sidhe	162
Cycles of Nature and Spirit	163
Death and Memory	163
Reflection	164

PART THREE: ATLAS OF AFTERLIFE COSMOLOGIES

A CARTOGRAPHY OF THE INVISIBLE	169

TYPE A: THE CYCLICAL COSMOS

HINDUISM: THE FOURTEEN-FOLD LADDER OF BEING	173
CLASSICAL BUDDHISM (THERAVĀDA): THE FLAME WITHOUT A WICK	177
TIBETAN BUDDHISM (VAJRAYĀNA): THE GEOGRAPHY OF THE IN-BETWEEN	181
JAINISM: THE PHYSICS OF SPIRITUAL GRAVITY	185

TYPE B: THE LINEAR-ASCENSION MODELS

ANCIENT EGYPT: THE WEIGHING OF THE HEART	191
THE GRECO-ROMAN MODEL: THE PEDAGOGICAL CYCLE	195
CHRISTIANITY (DANTE'S MODEL): THE CHRISTIAN MORAL GEOGRAPHY	199
KABBALAH (JUDAISM): THE ROLLING OF SOULS	203
SUFI ISLAM: THE ALCHEMY OF FANĀ' AND BAQĀ'	207

Type C: The Ancestral Continuum

The Celtic Tradition: The Ever-Living Ones	213
Yoruba Tradition: The Marketplace and the Home	217
The Akan Tradition: The Return of the Sunsum	221
Daoism & Chinese Folk Religion: The Bureaucracy of Hell	225
Shinto: The Way of the Kami	229
Reviewing the Map	234

Part Four: Finding Your Path

The Road Ahead	244
The 12 Unwholesome Cittas (Akusalacittāni)	246
The Core Distinctions:	247
Why "Prompting" Matters	247
A. Consciousness Rooted in Greed	249
B. Consciousness Rooted in Hatred	253
C. Consciousness Rooted in Delusion	254
How to Work With This List	256
Closing Thoughts	258

Appendix

Glossary	262
Index	266
About The Author	268
Continuing the Work: A Note on Alchemy	270

List of Illustrations

Unless otherwise stated, all images are reproduced from sources identified as public domain or Creative Commons Attribution licences. Many have been cropped, adjusted for contrast, or digitally enhanced using artificial-intelligence restoration tools for clarity and consistency of presentation.

These edits do not alter the original meaning or authorship of the works.

Zhuangzi	14th-century illustration from *The Ten Sons of Xuanmen* by Hua Zili, representing the Daoist sage whose writings celebrate transformation and the freedom of the spirit.
Pythagoras	'Do Not Eat Beans' (fol. 25 recto), pen & ink with watercolour, Woodner Collection, National Gallery of Art. A humorous allegory from the Pythagorean school on purity and discipline.
Empedocles	From *The History of Philosophy* (Thomas Stanley, 1655). Early modern engraving of the pre-Socratic philosopher who taught the four elements and the transmigration of souls.
Plato	Luni-marble copy by Silanion (c. 370 BCE), Sacred area in Largo Argentina, Rome.
Virgil	Modern bust by Tito Angelini in Vergiliano Park, Naples—Roman poet whose Aeneid imagines the soul's passage between lives.
Plutarch	Portrait of a philosopher (possibly Plutarch or Plotinus), 2nd century CE, Archaeological Museum of Delphi.
Plotinus	Marble head, Ostia Antica Museum (inv. 436). Founder of Neoplatonism; taught the soul's descent and return to the One.
Origen of Alexandria	Origene autore, manuscript of Schäftlarn (ca. 1160), Bayerische Staatsbibliothek, Munich.
The Druids / Julius Caesar	Portrait of Caesar by Ángel M. Felicísimo, Mérida, Spain—representing early Celtic belief in rebirth.
Giordano Bruno	Engraving, Wellcome Collection. Philosopher burned for asserting infinite worlds and recurring lives.
Gotthold Ephraim Lessing	Portrait by Anna Rosina de Gasc (c. 1767–68).
Benjamin Franklin	Painting by Joseph Duplessis (c. 1785), National Portrait Gallery.

XI

William Wordsworth	Portrait by William Souter (1798), Cornell University Libraries.
Arthur Schopenhauer	Photograph by Johann Schäfer (1859), Frankfurt am Main University Library.
Ralph Waldo Emerson	Albumen print by J. J. Hawes (1880 copy of 1857 daguerreotype).
W. B. Yeats	Photographic portrait by Alice Broughton.
Carl Jung	ETH-Bibliothek collection (c. 1935).
Aldous Huxley	Photograph from Life Magazine, 11 Jan 1954.
Timothy Leary	Portrait (public domain; no known restrictions).
Ram Dass	Portrait (public domain; no known restrictions).
George Harrison	Photo by David Hume Kennerly, Oval Office, 13 Dec 1974.
David Bowie	Stage photo during 1983 Serious Moonlight Tour by Jeffcat1.
Shirley MacLaine	Publicity photo from The Apartment (1960).
Camille Flammarion	Mr. Flammarion devant le globe de la planète Mars (1921), Bibliothèque nationale de France.
Thomas Edison	With early phonograph (c. 1877), Library of Congress.
Henry Ford	Studio portrait (25 May 1915), The Henry Ford Collections.
W. C. Alvarez	From Live at Peace With Your Nerves (1958), Prentice-Hall.
Albert Schweitzer	Photograph by Bundesarchiv Bild 183-D0116-0041-019.
Ian Stevenson	Photograph (public domain; no known restrictions).
Brian Weiss	Photo at Omega Institute (9 Oct 2012), author's own submission to Wikipedia.
Jim B. Tucker	Photograph by Dan Addison, University of Virginia.
Erlendur Haraldsson	Photograph (public domain; no known restrictions).
Satwant K. Pasricha	Photograph (public domain; no known restrictions).
Kamo no Chōmei	Portrait by Kikuchi Yōsai (菊池容斎).
Ramakrishna Paramahamsa	Photograph by Abinash Chandra Dna (Oct 1885).
Helena Blavatsky	Photograph (1877).
Annie Besant	London Stereoscopic Company photo, NYPL.

Sri Aurobindo & The Mother (Mirra Alfassa)	Sri Aurobindo (c. 1900) and India Post stamp of Mirra Alfassa (1978).
Paramahansa Yogananda	Photograph (c. 1920).
The 14th Dalai Lama	Photograph by Christopher Michel (2012).
Mahatma Gandhi	Studio photo (London 1931).
Winston Churchill	The Roaring Lion portrait by Yousuf Karsh (Dec 1941), Library and Archives Canada e010751643.
Rinpo-mon (Buddhism)	Modern mandala symbolising the Wheel of *Dharma* and interdependence.
Jain Prateek Chihna	Official Jain symbol adopted 1974—combines swastika, three dots, crescent, and hand of *ahiṃsā* to represent non-violence and liberation.
Kabbalistic Tree of Life	Diagram with Hebrew names of the Sephiroth—a map of emanations from the Divine.
Calligraphic "Allah"	Classical Islamic calligraphy symbolising divine unity and infinity.
Yoruba Tradition—Atúnwá	Illustration of the four cardinal points of the earth (2022) by Ìṣẹ̀ ṣe Assembly, depicting cyclic return (Atúnwá) and ancestral continuity.
Akan Tradition—Gye Nyame	Adinkra symbol meaning "Except for GOD," expressing the omnipotence of the Creator.
Khanda (Sikh Faith)	Double-edged sword with chakram and crossed kirpans—emblem of divine knowledge and temporal-spiritual balance.

All images are reproduced from sources identified as public domain or Creative Commons. Every effort has been made to confirm open-license status at the time of publication.

The infographic-style diagrams throughout this book were drafted using *NotebookLM* to organise structural ideas and ensure consistency across sections. All final visuals were refined, redrawn, and edited in *Pixelmator Pro* to align with the overall design and format of the print edition.

PUBLIC DOMAIN. SOURCE: WIKIMEDIA COMMONS (URL AVAILABLE ON REQUEST).

List of Tables

Table: 1. The Anatomy of the Soul	167
Table: 2. The Map of Hindu Realms	176
Table: 3. The Map of Buddhist Realms	179
Table: 4. The Map of Realms (The Six Bardos)	183
Table 5. The Map of Jain Realms	187
Table 6. The Map of Egyptian Realms	193
Table 7. The Map of Greco-Roman Realms	197
Table 8. The Map of Dante's Realms	201
Table 9. The Map of Kabbalistic Realms	205
Table 10. The Map of Islamic Realms	209
Table 11. The Map of Celtic Realms	215
Table 12. The Map of Yorubic Realms	219
Table 13. The Map of Akan Realms	223
Table 14. The Map of Daoist Realms	227
Table 15. The Map of Shinto Realms	231
Table 16. Reviewing The Systems and Models	234
Table 17. Synthesis – The Comparative Atlas	235
Table 18. The Twelve Unwholesome Citta	248

INTRODUCTION
Mapping the Invisible

THERE IS A QUESTION THAT HAUNTS THE EDGES OF EVERY HUMAN LIFE. It is whispered at bedsides, debated in academies, and chanted in temples across the world. It is the question that drives our philosophy and defines our courage: *What happens next?*

For most of us, the answer we hold is inherited. We are born into a story —a linear path to heaven, a cyclical return to earth, or perhaps a sudden stop into silence. We rarely look at the other maps. We assume that the geography of death is fixed, defined by the culture that raised us.

But what if we laid the maps side by side?

You, Again is an atlas of the invisible. It is an attempt to survey the topography of the afterlife not through the lens of a single faith, but through the collective imagination of humanity. From the high rises of Hindu cosmology to the bureaucratic tribunals of Chinese folk religion; from the psychological in-between states of Tibet to the ancestral villages of West Africa—we find that the human vision of death is startlingly diverse, yet profoundly connected.

In these pages, you will not find a sermon. You will not be asked to believe in a specific dogma. Instead, you will meet the diverse chorus of voices that have taken the idea of continuity seriously. You will hear from Greek philosophers and Roman poets, quantum physicists and Victorian psychiatrists, Sufi mystics and American transcendentalists.

They do not all agree on the details. Some see the soul as a prisoner seeking escape; others as a student seeking a lesson; still others as a volunteer returning to serve. But they share a single, resilient intuition: that human life is not a biological accident that ends in a blackout, but a chapter in a much longer story.

This book is divided into four parts:

- PART ONE: Establishes the possibility, looking at the sheer breadth of minds who have entertained the idea of rebirth.
- PART TWO: Profiles the specific voices—the wise and glorious—who have championed this view across history.
- PART THREE: Is the Atlas itself: a comparative look at the *physics* of the afterlife across different traditions.
- PART FOUR: Turns the lens inward, offering a practical framework for navigating the only terrain we can directly control: the landscape of our own minds right now.

Whether you are a skeptic, a seeker, or simply curious, I invite you to walk through these varying landscapes with an open mind. You may find that the map you were given is not the only one guiding the way home.

The *Flammarion* engraving is a wood engraving by an unknown artist that first appeared in Camille Flammarion's *L'Atmosphère: Météorologie populaire* (1888).
The image depicts a man crawling under the edge of the sky, depicted as if it were a solid hemisphere, to look at the mysterious Empyrean beyond. The caption underneath the engraving (not shown here) translates to "*A medieval missionary tells that he has found the point where heaven and Earth meet...*"

—Wikipedia.

This file has been identified as being free of known restrictions under copyright law, including all related and neighbouring rights.

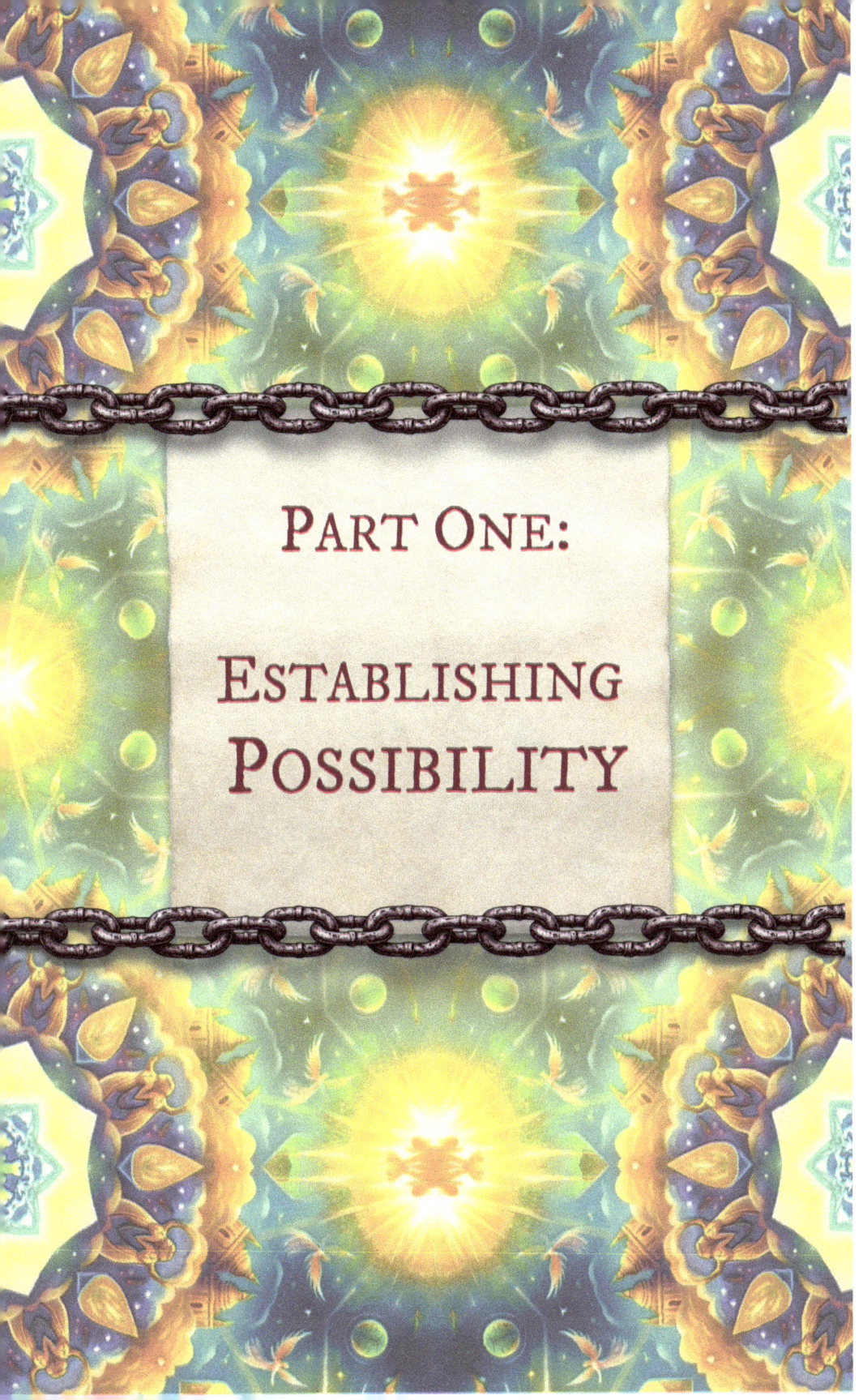

ASK THE WISE

I DID NOT ALWAYS TAKE THE IDEA OF REINCARNATION SERIOUSLY. FOR most of my life, I filed it away as an exotic belief—something for Hinduism, Buddhism, or other faiths of the *Indian sub-continent.* Interesting, perhaps, but not something for me.

That changed after two decades of research and study. Over the last few years I began reading more deeply in the writings of philosophers from antiquity.

To my surprise, I found ideas that resonated not only with Buddhism and Kabbalah but also with the Christianity I was raised to understand. These were not the musings of dreamers or the credulous. They were the thoughts of rational, disciplined, and often brilliant minds.

This section is not here to argue that reincarnation is true. It is here simply to demonstrate that some of the finest thinkers—philosophers, poets, mystics, scientists—have considered it a serious possibility. If such a diverse array of rational and intelligent people thought rebirth worthy of attention, then perhaps the rest of us should at least be curious.

Of course, attitudes toward religion vary widely. Some approach anything religious with suspicion, if not hostility. Often, this is not without reason: history provides no shortage of abuses carried out in the name of faith. But to turn away from all religion may also mean discarding teachings that could be deeply helpful. The doctrine of reincarnation may be one such teaching.

Even the mere belief that rebirth is possible can change how one lives.

It gives purpose and direction. It encourages curiosity. Over time, it even softens the fear of death. To remain ignorant, by contrast, is to surrender the opportunity of this rare opportunity of human birth. Buddhist texts compare it to the odds of a blind turtle, surfacing once every hundred years, happening to put its head through a single yoke floating on the vast ocean. To be human is that rare—and perhaps, that precious.

So, with curiosity as our guide, let us meet those who have taken reincarnation seriously. Across cultures and centuries, they speak with one voice: that life is not a single spark in the dark, but part of a continuing stream.

Philosophers and Classical Voices

The trail begins in China, with Zhuangzi (c. 369–286 BCE), the Daoist sage who delighted in turning logic upside down. To him, life and death were simply transformations of breath—gathered and dispersed in cycles.

"Why lament?" he asked. "This is the eternal returning." He was perhaps the first to suggest that rebirth need not be frightening; it is as natural as the inhaling and exhaling of the cosmos itself.

Meanwhile, in Greece, Pythagoras (c. 570–495 BCE) was making his followers swear off beans, tune lyres, and reflect on their immortal souls. Herodotus tells us Pythagoras believed the soul passed through many lives, sometimes in human form, sometimes in animal. For him, mathematics and Metempsychōsis belonged to the same cosmic order: harmony was not only in numbers, but in the cycle of birth and rebirth.His successor Empedocles (c. 494–434 BCE) took the matter personally: "I have been a boy and a girl, a bush and a bird, and a dumb fish in the sea." His confession reminds us that reincarnation was not abstract theory but an existential reality.

With Plato (429–347 BCE), reincarnation became a matter of philosophical prestige. In the *Phaedo*, Socrates recalls the "ancient tradition" that souls are born from the dead. In the *Republic*, he gives us the *Myth of Er*, where souls choose their next lives before returning to the world. Plato's testimony ensured that rebirth was stitched into the very fabric of Western philosophy.

The Romans added poetry to the mix. Virgil (70–19 BCE), in the *Aeneid*, describes souls drinking from the river *Lethe* to forget their past lives before returning to earth. For centuries this text was a required reading in schools—meaning generations of Roman (and later European) students were taught that reincarnation was part of the classical canon.

From the philosopher-poet we move to the philosopher-priest.

Plutarch (c. 46–120 CE), writing as a priest of Apollo, taught that divine justice works itself out across multiple lives. The soul's punishment or reward may be postponed, but it is never forgotten.

His near contemporary Plotinus (204–270 CE), founder of Neoplatonism, also saw reincarnation as part of the soul's ascent and descent. "Socrates' soul comes to be different individuals at different times," he wrote. For Plotinus, rebirth was woven into the soul's journey back to the One.

Even Christianity's early thinkers were not immune. Origen of Alexandria (c. 184–253 CE) speculated that souls pre-exist before entering the body and might descend or rise again according to virtue. Later condemned, his views still show how porous the boundaries were between Greek philosophy and Christian theology.

Meanwhile, in the misty groves of Gaul, the Druids were teaching much the same. Julius Caesar reports that they believed souls do not perish but pass from one to another. For them, reincarnation was not abstract but central to their moral and religious order.

Centuries later, Giordano Bruno (1548–1600), Renaissance visionary and martyr for infinity, proclaimed that souls pass from one being to another—part of a universe without end. For that, among other heresies, he was burned alive in Rome.

The Enlightenment, often thought allergic to mystical ideas, gave us Lessing (1729–1781). "Why should I not come back more than once?" he asked in *The Education of the Human Race*. If GOD educates souls, why would He not use more than one lifetime?

Even America's practical-minded Benjamin Franklin (1706–1790) toyed with the idea. His youthful epitaph reads like a publisher's joke: the body, he said, is "food for worms," but the "work shall not be wholly lost… it will appear once more in a new and more perfect Edition." Franklin, as always, found a witty way to say something serious.

The Romantics, too, were smitten. Wordsworth (1770–1850) wrote that "our birth is but a sleep and a forgetting," as though we come from afar with memories half intact.

Schopenhauer (1788–1860), deeply influenced by the Upanishads, gave reincarnation a new philosophical term—*"palingenesis"*—and argued that rebirth was a central truth of existence.

In America, Ralph Waldo Emerson (1803–1882) affirmed that the soul is immortal and "passes into other habitations."

W.B. Yeats (1865–1939), Irish poet and occultist, was blunt: "I am certain that I have been a monk in Salamanca. And I am certain that I was once, perhaps many times, a woman." Carl Jung (1875–1961), the psychologist, called reincarnation a "most probable hypothesis."

Aldous Huxley (1894–1963), the philosopher-novelist, thought it the only doctrine that made sense of both justice and freedom.

Timothy Leary (1920–1996) reinterpreted reincarnation in countercultural terms—"you're only as young as the last time you changed your mind."

And finally, Ram Dass (1931–2019), Harvard psychologist turned spiritual teacher, declared: "I am not this body. I am not this role. I am a soul. As such, I have lived thousands of lives and will live thousands more until I am free."

Artists, Scientists, and Saints

The chorus grows louder when we add artists and musicians (George Harrison, David Bowie, Shirley MacLaine), scientists and inventors (Edison, Ford, Flammarion), physicians (Schweitzer, Stevenson, Tucker, Pasricha), and mystics and reformers (Ramakrishna, Yogananda, the Dalai Lama, Gandhi). Each in their own way affirmed that life is a stream, not a snapshot.

World Religions and Traditions

Finally, whole traditions join the chorus: Hinduism and Buddhism, Jainism and Kabbalah, Sufi Islam, the Yoruba and Akan of West Africa, and even the Japanese recluse Kamo no Chōmei. All, in their own languages and metaphors, insist that souls return—for learning, for justice, for liberation.

Reflection

From China to India, Greece to Gaul, Enlightenment Europe to modern America, across Africa and Japan—the idea of reincarnation keeps resurfacing. The voices differ in tone: some poetic, some philosophical, some mystical, some scientific. Yet they agree on one point: life does not end with one body, one birth, or one death.

This does not prove reincarnation. But it does prove that the idea is no idle fancy. It has appealed to some of the most brilliant minds and most enduring traditions. And if so many have found it worthy of thought, perhaps curiosity alone demands that we do the same.

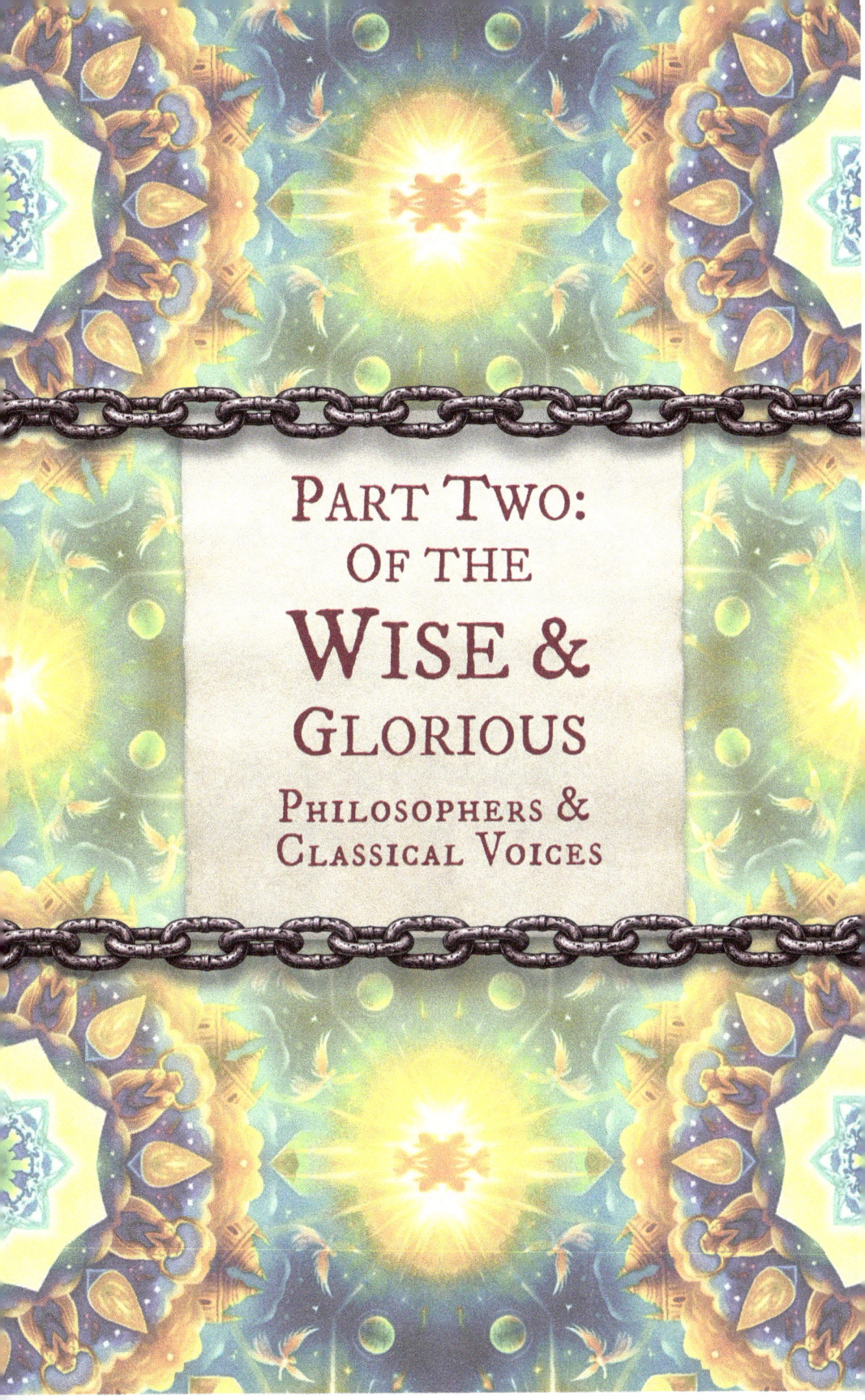

You Again

ZHUANGZI (C. 369–286 BCE)

Born	State of Song, China
Died	c. 286 BCE, China
Profession	Daoist philosopher, writer
Known For	*Zhuangzi* (Daoist classic text)

ZHUANGZI WAS ONE OF THE TWO GREAT FOUNDERS OF DAOISM, alongside Laozi. Where Laozi offered aphorisms in the *Dao De Jing*, Zhuangzi delighted in stories, paradoxes, and playful dialogues that revealed the relativity of all perspectives. His writings often blur dream and reality, life and death, making him one of the most radical voices in world philosophy.

He saw life and death not as opposites, but as transformations within the flow of the *Dao*. Just as the seasons turn and rivers shift course, so the breath that constitutes life gathers and disperses. In this view, what we call 'death' is no more tragic than the setting of the sun—it is a continuation in another form.

Zhuangzi's reflections on transformation have been described as one of the earliest Chinese expressions of rebirth. His butterfly dream—waking unsure whether he was a man who dreamed of being a butterfly, or a butterfly dreaming of being a man—captures his conviction that identity itself is fluid and changeable. This vision of rebirth as transformation shaped Daoist and

Chinese thought for centuries, embedding the idea of eternal return into East Asian philosophy and inspiring poets, painters, and mystics alike.

> "Life is a loan from the gathered breath. Death is the dispersal of the same. When breath gathers, it is life; when it scatters, it is death. Why lament? This is the eternal returning."
>
> — *ZHUANGZI* (BOOK 18)

> "Once Zhuang Zhou dreamed he was a butterfly... He did not know if he was Zhou who had dreamed of being a butterfly, or a butterfly dreaming that he was Zhou. Between Zhou and the butterfly there must be some distinction! This is called the transformation of things."
>
> — *ZHUANGZI* (BOOK 2)

Zhuangzi's refusal to mourn death, his ease with transformation, and his humour in facing the great unknown make him a distinctive early voice for rebirth. In his vision, to live is to flow with change; to die is simply to flow on.

PYTHAGORAS (C. 570–495 BCE)

BORN	SAMOS, GREECE
DIED	METAPONTUM, ITALY
PROFESSION	PHILOSOPHER; MATHEMATICIAN; RELIGIOUS TEACHER
KNOWN FOR	PYTHAGOREAN THEOREM; FOUNDING PHILOSOPHICAL–RELIGIOUS COMMUNITY

PYTHAGORAS IS REMEMBERED TODAY FOR THE THEOREM THAT BEARS his name, but in antiquity he was revered as a sage, mystic, and the founder of a way of life. He established a disciplined community in Croton, southern Italy, that combined mathematics, ritual purity, music, and philosophy. His followers lived under strict rules, including vegetarianism and periods of silence, treating numbers as sacred principles and music as a reflection of cosmic harmony.

Central to Pythagoras's teaching was the immortality and transmigration of the soul. Ancient sources testify that he declared the soul passes through many lives—human, animal, and even plant. This belief was no minor speculation: it was woven into the Pythagorean ethic of nonviolence, purity, and respect for all living beings.

Herodotus, writing in the 5th century BCE, noted that Pythagoras and his followers taught "that the soul of man is immortal, and that when the body dies it enters into another creature which is then born; and after passing through all creatures of land, sea, and air, it enters again into the body of a man" (*Histories* 2.123–4). Ovid, centuries later, placed the same doctrine into

You Again

Pythagoras's mouth in the *Metamorphoses*: "All things change, nothing dies; the soul wanders, arriving now here, now there, taking possession of whatever body it pleases" (*Metamorphoses 15.165–67*).

For Pythagoras, mathematics and reincarnation belonged to the same order of truth: both revealed a universe structured by harmony and governed by eternal law. His legacy ensured that the idea of rebirth entered Western philosophy not as myth but as a rational principle.

> "He declared the soul was immortal; that it changes into other kinds of living things."
> — Herodotus, *Histories 2.123–4*

> "All things change; nothing dies. The spirit wanders... it enters another body, but always remains the same."
> — Ovid, *Metamorphoses 15.165–67*

EMPEDOCLES (C. 494–434 BCE)

Born	Acragas, Sicily
Died	c. 434 BCE
Profession	Philosopher; poet; physician
Known For	Theories of the four elements; cosmic forces of Love and Strife

Empedocles was one of the most dazzling figures of Greek antiquity—at once philosopher, poet, mystic, and healer. He wrote in epic verse, blending scientific speculation with religious vision. His cosmology proposed that all things are composed of four eternal "roots"—earth, air, fire, and water—bound together and torn apart by the opposing forces of Love (*philia*) and Strife (*neikos*). This vision of a universe in perpetual transformation placed Empedocles among the most original thinkers of the pre-Socratic age.

But Empedocles was not content with abstract theory. He claimed to have lived many lives in many forms, an explicit confession of reincarnation that makes him one of the earliest Western voices to testify to the soul's transmigration. His fragmentary poems include the striking self-revelation:

> "For I have been ere now a boy and a girl,
> a bush and a bird, and a dumb fish in the sea."
>
> — *Fragment B117*

His declaration suggests not mere speculation but personal memory—an identity that has wandered through countless births. This belief was tied to his ethic of purity and nonviolence: Empedocles urged vegetarianism, abstention from blood sacrifice, and compassion for all beings, for each creature might once have been kin.

Later sources describe him as a wonder-worker and healer, performing miracles and claiming semi-divine status. Whether history or legend, his life became a symbol of philosophy as lived practice, where the boundary between human and divine, life and death, was porous.

Empedocles' insistence on the cycle of rebirth was not a marginal doctrine but central to his moral and cosmic vision. His words echo through later Platonism, Neoplatonism, and even modern vegetarian movements, reminding us that reincarnation once stood at the heart of philosophy itself.

PLATO (429–347 BCE)

BORN	ATHENS, GREECE
DIED	ATHENS, GREECE
PROFESSION	PHILOSOPHER; FOUNDER OF THE ACADEMY
KNOWN FOR	DIALOGUES; THEORY OF FORMS; INFLUENCE ON WESTERN PHILOSOPHY

PLATO, STUDENT OF SOCRATES AND TEACHER OF ARISTOTLE, IS ONE OF the most influential thinkers in history. His dialogues shaped the very foundations of Western philosophy, ranging across ethics, politics, metaphysics, and the nature of the soul. Central to his thought was the conviction that life does not end at death but continues in cycles of rebirth.

In the *Phaedo*, Socrates refers to the "ancient tradition" that the souls of the dead return to the living:

> "There is an ancient tradition… that the souls of the dead are in existence, and that the living come from them."
> — *PHAEDO 72E*

Later in the same dialogue, Socrates argues that philosophy is a preparation for death precisely because the soul survives and returns.

In the *Republic*, Plato sets out the famous *Myth of Er* (Book 10). Here, Er, slain in battle, returns to life to tell what he has seen: souls awaiting rebirth, choosing their next lives, and drinking from the river *Lethe* to forget their former existence before returning to earth. This myth became one of the most enduring Western visions of reincarnation:

> "After they had all chosen their lives, they proceeded in order to *Lachesis.* And each received from her the destiny he had chosen, which was bound by her hand as the thread of fate. Then they passed beneath the throne of *Necessity*... and so, in due time, they came to birth."
>
> — *Republic X*, 620E–621B

Plato also alludes to transmigration in other dialogues, including the *Meno* and *Timaeus*, suggesting that learning itself may be a recollection of truths the soul has known in former lives.

Because of Plato's unparalleled authority in the Western canon, his testimony gave reincarnation intellectual legitimacy for centuries. Later philosophers, Christian theologians, and poets inherited his imagery of the soul's cycles, whether to affirm or to refute it. His vision ensured that rebirth was not confined to myth or religion but became a respectable theme of philosophy itself.

VIRGIL (70–19 BCE)

BORN	ANDES, NEAR MANTUA, ITALY
DIED	BRUNDISIUM, ITALY
PROFESSION	POET
KNOWN FOR	*THE AENEID*—ROME'S NATIONAL EPIC

PUBLIUS VERGILIUS MARO, better known as Virgil, was Rome's greatest poet. His works—especially *The Aeneid*—became the literary backbone of Roman education and culture, studied by generations of schoolboys throughout the Empire and the Middle Ages. Within this national epic, Virgil gave one of antiquity's most vivid poetic accounts of reincarnation.

In Book VI of *The Aeneid*, the Trojan hero Aeneas descends into the underworld, where his father Anchises reveals the fate of souls. After death, Anchises explains, spirits are purged of their stains, then drink from the river *Lethe* to forget their past lives before returning to the world above:

> "All these souls... drink the waters of *Lethe's* stream,
> so that they may revisit the vault above,
> and begin once more to long for the body."
>
> — *AENEID* VI.713–715

Here reincarnation is woven into Roman cosmology itself: a cycle of purification, forgetting, and rebirth. Virgil's vision was not an esoteric doctrine but part of the central text of Latin education. Every literate Roman

—and later, every medieval European scholar—encountered reincarnation in the pages of their most authoritative poet.

Later traditions, from Dante's *Divine Comedy* to Renaissance humanism, drew heavily on Virgil's imagery. The *Lethe*, in particular, became a symbol of forgetfulness before rebirth in Christian and secular literature alike.

By placing reincarnation at the heart of Rome's founding epic, Virgil ensured that the idea was transmitted not as marginal speculation but as part of the cultural canon of Europe. His lines made rebirth an imaginative and poetic certainty for centuries of readers.

PLUTARCH (C. 46–120 CE)

BORN	CHAERONEA, BOEOTIA, GREECE
DIED	DELPHI, GREECE
PROFESSION	BIOGRAPHER; ESSAYIST; PLATONIST; PHILOSOPHER
KNOWN FOR	*PARALLEL LIVES; MORALIA*

PLUTARCH WAS ONE OF THE MOST WIDELY READ AUTHORS OF antiquity. His *Parallel Lives* paired Greek and Roman statesmen as moral examples, shaping biography as a literary form. His *Moralia* gathered essays on philosophy, religion, and ethics, blending Platonic philosophy with practical wisdom. Serving as a priest of Apollo at Delphi, he straddled the worlds of religion and philosophy, making him a respected cultural authority across the Empire.

Reincarnation appears in his writings as part of divine justice. In *On the Delay of Divine Justice* (567D–F), Plutarch explains that punishment and reward do not always arrive in one lifetime. Instead, the soul's destiny unfolds across multiple incarnations:

> "The punishment of the soul is postponed, and it is transferred to another body to undergo what it deserves."
> — *ON THE DELAY OF DIVINE JUSTICE* 567D–F

Elsewhere, in *On the Face in the Moon* (a curious essay blending cosmology and myth), Plutarch describes the soul's ascent and descent between bodies, with the moon acting as a way-station in its journey. These writings reveal his conviction that *metempsychōsis* was not an exotic speculation but part of the moral order of the cosmos.

For Plutarch, reincarnation solved a perennial problem: why do the wicked prosper and the good suffer? Justice, he argued, stretches beyond the boundaries of one life. The soul carries its debts and credits forward until balance is achieved.

Because Plutarch's works were widely read through late antiquity, the Renaissance, and into the modern era, his voice helped keep the idea of rebirth alive in Western moral and religious thought. His testimony shows that for educated Greeks and Romans, reincarnation was not fringe mysticism but integrated into mainstream philosophy and theology.

PLOTINUS (204–270 CE)

BORN	LYCOPOLIS, EGYPT
DIED	CAMPANIA, ITALY
PROFESSION	PHILOSOPHER; FOUNDER OF NEOPLATONISM
KNOWN FOR	*THE ENNEADS*; PROFOUND INFLUENCE ON CHRISTIAN AND ISLAMIC PHILOSOPHY

PLOTINUS STANDS AT THE CROSSROADS OF PHILOSOPHY AND mysticism. A student of Ammonius Saccas in Alexandria, he later founded his own school in Rome. His teachings, compiled by his disciple Porphyry as The Enneads, became the foundation of Neoplatonism—a system that shaped late antiquity, early Christianity, Islamic philosophy, and the Renaissance.

For Plotinus, all reality emanates from the ineffable One—the source of being and goodness. The human soul, a spark of this divine source, descends into bodies and rises again through purification and contemplation. Reincarnation was therefore a natural corollary of his metaphysics: the soul, caught between matter and spirit, takes on new forms until it returns to its source.

Plotinus remarks:

> "Socrates' soul comes to be different individuals at different times, say Pythagoras or someone else."
>
> — *ENNEADS* IV.3

Elsewhere he suggests that the form of reincarnation depends on the moral state of the soul: noble souls may ascend quickly, while degraded ones fall into lower forms of life. In his vision, rebirth was not arbitrary but part of a cosmic pedagogy, shaping the soul's journey toward ultimate union with the One.

Plotinus also offered a distinctive psychology of memory and identity: while the outer personality dissolves, the true self—the immortal rational soul—endures across incarnations. This allowed him to integrate ethical responsibility, cosmic justice, and mystical ascent within a single system.

Through Neoplatonism, his vision of reincarnation influenced early Christian thinkers (sometimes indirectly), Islamic philosophers like Avicenna and Renaissance Platonists such as Marsilio Ficino. His insistence that rebirth belongs to the soul's cosmic rhythm gave the doctrine a philosophical dignity that reverberated across centuries.

ORIGEN OF ALEXANDRIA (C. 184–253 CE)

BORN	ALEXANDRIA, EGYPT
DIED	TYRE, ROMAN SYRIA
PROFESSION	CHRISTIAN THEOLOGIAN; SCHOLAR; CHURCH FATHER
KNOWN FOR	*ON FIRST PRINCIPLES*; BIBLICAL EXEGESIS; FOUNDING EARLY CHRISTIAN THEOLOGY

ORIGEN WAS ONE OF THE MOST BRILLIANT AND PROLIFIC MINDS OF the early Church. A tireless biblical commentator and philosopher, he sought to harmonise Greek philosophy with Christian revelation. His ideas were so bold that he was revered as a genius by some and condemned as a heretic by others.

Central to his thought was the pre-existence of souls—the idea that rational beings existed with GOD before birth. In *On First Principles (I.6.3)*, he describes how souls fall away from divine contemplation and take on bodies suited to their condition:

> "All rational creatures who are incorporeal and invisible, if they become negligent, gradually sink into lower conditions, and take for themselves bodies first ethereal, then aerial, and finally human flesh."
>
> — *ON FIRST PRINCIPLES* I.6.3

This teaching implied that embodiment was not a one-time event but part of a larger cycle of descent and possible return. While Origen explicitly denied the Greek doctrine of transmigration in its cruder forms, his speculations opened the door to thinking of life as one episode in a much longer journey of the soul.

His views were controversial. Later Church councils condemned the doctrine of pre-existence and any hint of reincarnation, declaring resurrection (not transmigration) as the Christian hope. Yet Origen's writings reveal how porous the boundaries were between Hellenistic philosophy and early Christian theology.

Origen's willingness to consider rebirth as a moral process—souls descending or rising according to virtue—shows that reincarnation was not unthinkable even within the formative centuries of Christianity. His intellectual daring influenced later mystics and esoteric Christians, keeping alive the possibility that the soul's story may stretch far beyond a single earthly life.

THE DRUIDS (AS REPORTED BY JULIUS CAESAR)

SOURCE:	GAUL, 1ST CENTURY BCE
PROFESSION	PRIESTS; PHILOSOPHERS OF THE CELTIC TRIBES
KNOWN FOR	ORAL TEACHING; SACRED GROVES; MEDIATING LAW, WAR, AND RELIGION

THE DRUIDS WERE THE SPIRITUAL ELITE OF THE CELTIC WORLD. They served as judges, teachers, astronomers, and priests, preserving their knowledge orally rather than in writing. While much of what we know comes from Roman observers, the testimony is consistent: reincarnation lay at the very heart of their teaching.

Julius Caesar, writing in *The Gallic War (6.14)*, reports:

> "The Druids... wish to inculcate this as one of their leading beliefs, that souls do not perish, but pass after death from one to another."
>
> — *GALLIC WAR* 6.14

Other classical authors confirmed the same. Diodorus Siculus noted that the Celts believed in the "immortality of the soul" and its passage into new bodies. Lucan, the Roman poet, described the Druids as teaching that death was but "a passageway" to another life (*Pharsalia I.454–457*).

For the Celts, this doctrine was not mere speculation but a moral cornerstone. Belief in rebirth gave courage in battle, since warriors saw death as a transition rather than an end. It also underpinned ethics and law, binding actions to consequences beyond a single lifetime.

The Druids' conviction shows that reincarnation was not limited to India, Greece, or the Near East, but was also embedded in the lived religion of ancient Europe. Their teachings, passed on through oral tradition, reveal a striking convergence: across continents, wise teachers told their people that the soul does not perish but returns again and again.

OF THE WISE & GLORIOUS

GIORDANO BRUNO (1548–1600)

BORN	NOLA, ITALY
DIED	ROME, ITALY
PROFESSION	PHILOSOPHER; DOMINICAN FRIAR, COSMOLOGIST
KNOWN FOR	VISION OF INFINITE WORLDS; DEFIANCE OF CHURCH ORTHODOXY

GIORDANO BRUNO WAS ONE OF THE BOLDEST THINKERS OF THE Renaissance—a Dominican friar who broke beyond the limits of medieval cosmology. He championed the idea of an infinite universe filled with countless stars and worlds, each animated by its own life. For this cosmic vision, combined with his outspoken rejection of orthodoxy, he was condemned by the Inquisition and burned alive in Rome's Campo de' Fiori in 1600.

Reincarnation was central to Bruno's philosophy. He explicitly taught the transmigration of souls as part of the universe's perpetual cycle of transformation:

> "The soul is not extinguished, but, after leaving the body, passes from one living being to another."
>
> — *ON THE CAUSE, THE PRINCIPLE, AND THE ONE* (1584)

For Bruno, rebirth was not a punishment but an affirmation of the soul's eternal vitality within a boundless cosmos. Just as matter changes form without ceasing to exist, so too the soul journeys from one body to another, woven into the fabric of infinity.

His doctrine drew on Pythagorean and Platonic traditions but was expanded to match his radical vision of infinite worlds. Every soul, like every star, belonged to an endless order of renewal.

Bruno's embrace of reincarnation reveals how Renaissance philosophy wove together mysticism, science, and courage. His martyrdom ensured that he would be remembered not only as a cosmologist of infinity but as one of Europe's most defiant witnesses to the immortality and return of the soul.

GOTTHOLD EPHRAIM LESSING (1729–1781)

BORN KAMENZ, SAXONY (GERMANY)

DIED BRUNSWICK, GERMANY

PROFESSION PHILOSOPHER; DRAMATIST; CRITIC

KNOWN FOR *NATHAN THE WISE; THE EDUCATION OF THE HUMAN RACE*

LESSING WAS ONE OF THE GREAT MINDS OF THE GERMAN ENLIGHTENment—a playwright, philosopher, and critic who fought for freedom of thought and religious tolerance. His drama *Nathan the Wise* (1779), with its parable of the three rings, became an early manifesto for interfaith respect. In philosophy, he sought to reconcile reason with faith, anticipating themes of both Romanticism and modern liberal theology.

In his late work *The Education of the Human Race* (1780), Lessing turned explicitly to reincarnation. He argued that just as humanity develops gradually through history, so too do individual souls advance through repeated lives. For him, rebirth was a rational solution to the problem of spiritual growth:

> "Why should I not come back more than once? Is this life so complete, so finished, that there is no room for another?"
>
> — *THE EDUCATION OF THE HUMAN RACE*, §§95–98

He presented reincarnation not as mystical fancy but as divine pedagogy. God, he reasoned, educates the soul as a teacher educates a pupil—not in one lesson, but in many. Each lifetime offers another chapter in this long schooling.

Lessing's formulation gave reincarnation a place in Enlightenment thought, a period often associated with scepticism toward the supernatural. By framing it as a rational hypothesis about divine justice and human perfectibility, he bridged the gulf between mysticism and reason.

His influence was wide: later German Romantics, Theosophists, and even modern spiritual seekers found inspiration in his vision of a God who teaches through lifetimes. Lessing stands as proof that reincarnation could appeal not only to mystics and poets but also to the most rigorous rationalists of the modern age.

BENJAMIN FRANKLIN (1706–1790)

BORN	BOSTON, MASSACHUSETTS, USA
DIED	PHILADELPHIA, PENNSYLVANIA, USA
PROFESSION	STATESMAN; INVENTOR; SCIENTIST, WRITER
KNOWN FOR	FOUNDING FATHER OF THE UNITED STATES; ELECTRICITY EXPERIMENTS; DIPLOMACY; *POOR RICHARD'S ALMANACK*

BENJAMIN FRANKLIN WAS ONE OF THE MOST PRACTICAL AND inventive figures of the Enlightenment. Printer, scientist, diplomat, and statesman, he helped draft both the Declaration of Independence and the U.S. Constitution. Yet behind the pragmatist and wit stood a man unafraid to speculate about the immortality of the soul.

As a young man of 23 Franklin composed an epitaph for himself in the playful style of a printer's notice. In it, he imagined his body as a worn-out book—food for worms—but promised a new, improved edition:

> "The Body of B. Franklin, Printer;
> Like the Cover of an old Book,
> Its Contents torn out,
> And stript of its Lettering and Gilding,
> Lies here, Food for Worms.
> But the Work shall not be wholly lost;
> For it will, as he believ'd, appear once more,
> In a new & more perfect Edition,
> Corrected and amended by the Author."
>
> — FRANKLIN'S EPITAPH (C. 1728)

You Again

Although half-humorous, the epitaph reveals his youthful conviction in reincarnation. Later in life, Franklin confirmed he had long believed in the transmigration of souls. Writing to the theologian George Whitefield, he admitted that while he was unsure of the details of the afterlife, he leaned toward the idea that the soul continues to return in new forms.

Franklin's embrace of the doctrine is striking because of his reputation as a man of science and state. If even the hard-headed inventor of the lightning rod entertained reincarnation, then the idea could hardly be dismissed as irrational or the province of mystics alone. His epitaph, still read today, reminds us that rebirth can be imagined not only as a mystical doctrine but also as a witty, hopeful affirmation of the soul's resilience.

WILLIAM WORDSWORTH (1770–1850)

BORN	COCKERMOUTH, ENGLAND
DIED	RYDAL MOUNT, ENGLAND
PROFESSION	POET
KNOWN FOR	LYRICAL BALLADS; ROMANTIC POETRY OF NATURE AND MEMORY

WILLIAM WORDSWORTH, ONE OF THE FOUNDERS OF ENGLISH Romanticism, gave poetic voice to the spiritual depth of nature and the inner life. His verse sought to reveal the eternal in the everyday, blending personal reflection with cosmic suggestion. Nowhere is this clearer than in his great Ode: *Intimations of Immortality from Recollections of Early Childhood* (1807), where he sets forth a vision of pre-existence and rebirth that became a cornerstone of Romantic spirituality.

The ode famously begins with the haunting assertion:

> "Our birth is but a sleep and a forgetting:
> The Soul that rises with us, our life's Star,
> Hath had elsewhere its setting,
> And cometh from afar…"
>
> — *ODE: INTIMATIONS OF IMMORTALITY* (1807)

Here, Wordsworth suggests that children arrive in this world already touched by eternity—bearing faint memories of another life. As we grow older, those memories fade, yet the sense of having "come from afar" lingers in the depths of the heart.

This doctrine of the soul's pre-existence was not lifted from any one tradition but seems to emerge from Wordsworth's own profound sense of continuity in nature. The cycles of seasons, rivers, and mountains suggested to him a spiritual cycle that embraced human life as well. For Wordsworth, reincarnation was less a dogma than a poetic truth: the soul belongs to a continuum larger than one earthly span.

The Ode became one of the defining texts of English Romanticism, inspiring poets, philosophers, and theologians alike. By clothing the idea of rebirth in sublime imagery, Wordsworth ensured that reincarnation entered the Western imagination not as philosophy or theology, but as poetry that spoke to the heart.

ARTHUR SCHOPENHAUER (1788–1860)

Born	Danzig (Gdańsk), Poland
Died	Frankfurt am Main, Germany
Profession	Philosopher
Known For	*The World as Will and Representation*; influence on Nietzsche and Freud

Arthur Schopenhauer was the great pessimist of modern philosophy—yet his vision of reality drew deeply from Eastern thought. He was among the first major European philosophers to study the *Upaniṣads* and early Buddhist texts, which he encountered through Latin and German translations. Their influence was profound: he kept a copy of the *Upaniṣads* by his bedside, calling them "the solace of my life and the solace of my death."

From these sources he adopted the idea of rebirth, which he reframed in his own vocabulary as *palingenesis*. In his philosophy, the individual is a fleeting appearance of the underlying "Will"—a blind striving that manifests itself in countless forms. Death does not extinguish the Will; it simply reshapes itself into new lives.

In The World as Will and Representation, he writes:

> "In the succession of births... the persons who now stand in close connection will also be born along with us at the next birth."
>
> — *The World as Will and Representation, Supplement IV*

For Schopenhauer, reincarnation explained both the persistence of character and the injustices of existence. The suffering we experience is not random: it arises from the momentum of past actions and desires. He saw this as a metaphysical truth confirmed by the universality of the doctrine in ancient cultures.

Although bleak in tone, Schopenhauer's acceptance of rebirth gave his philosophy a spiritual dimension. He argued that only through renunciation, compassion, and ascetic insight could the Will be stilled—a vision remarkably close to Buddhist *nirvāṇa*.

His ideas influenced not only philosophers such as Nietzsche but also artists and musicians, including Richard Wagner and Thomas Mann. By importing reincarnation into the heart of modern Western philosophy, Schopenhauer gave the doctrine a rigorous, metaphysical framework that continues to resonate today.

RALPH WALDO EMERSON (1803–1882)

BORN	BOSTON, MASSACHUSETTS, USA
DIED	CONCORD, MASSACHUSETTS, USA
PROFESSION	ESSAYIST; PHILOSOPHER; POET
KNOWN FOR	ESSAYS; NATURE; LEADING FIGURE OF AMERICAN TRANSCENDENTALISM

RALPH WALDO EMERSON WAS THE GUIDING LIGHT OF AMERICAN Transcendentalism, a movement that sought to unite philosophy, poetry, and spirituality in a vision of divine unity. He drew inspiration from European Romanticism, Neoplatonism, and, increasingly, the sacred texts of India, which he encountered in translation. His writings reveal an explicit conviction in the immortality and rebirth of the soul.

In his essay *History* (1841), Emerson describes the soul's journey as continuous and eternal:

> "The soul comes from without into the human body, as into a temporary abode, and it goes out of it anew. It passes into other habitations, for the soul is immortal."
> — *ESSAYS: FIRST SERIES* (1841)

Elsewhere he makes the same claim with poetic brevity: "The soul is not born; it does not die; it was not produced from anyone; uncreated and imperishable, it is eternal"—echoing almost word for word the Hindu *Katha Upaniṣad* (a text he admired).

For Emerson, reincarnation was not superstition but natural law. Just as nature cycles through seasons and forms, so too does the soul. Each lifetime is a stage in its education, and death is but a door to new habitation.

This belief underpinned his broader philosophy of self-reliance and moral growth. If the soul continues, then every action, every act of courage or cowardice, contributes to an eternal curriculum. Rebirth, in Emerson's thought, is the guarantee that the universe is moral at its core—no effort is wasted, no lesson lost.

As the leading voice of America's literary and philosophical renaissance, Emerson gave reincarnation cultural authority in the New World. His words ensured that the doctrine entered not only esoteric circles but the mainstream of American literature and spirituality.

W.B. YEATS (1865–1939)

BORN	SANDYMOUNT, DUBLIN, IRELAND
DIED	MENTON, FRANCE
PROFESSION	POET; DRAMATIST; NOBEL LAUREATE
KNOWN FOR	*THE TOWER*; *THE SECOND COMING*; IRISH LITERARY REVIVAL

WILLIAM BUTLER YEATS, ONE OF THE GREATEST POETS OF THE 20th century, combined artistic genius with a lifelong fascination for mysticism, occultism, and reincarnation. As a founding member of the HERMETIC ORDER OF THE GOLDEN DAWN, he immersed himself in Western esotericism, and later in Theosophy and Indian philosophy. These influences coloured both his private writings and his poetry, shaping his personal mythology of history and of the soul.

Yeats did not treat reincarnation as an abstract idea: he claimed vivid memories of past lives. In his autobiographical writings, he confessed:

> "I am certain that I have been a monk in the great monastery at Salamanca. And I am certain that I was once, perhaps many times, a woman."
>
> — *AUTOBIOGRAPHIES* (1938)

In his visionary system, laid out in *A Vision* (1925, revised 1937), Yeats described history itself as cyclical, moving through vast gyres of time, with human souls reincarnating to play their part in the great spiral of destiny.

Rebirth for him was not merely personal but cosmic—an engine of both poetry and prophecy.

This conviction bled into his verse. In poems like *The Song of Wandering Aengus* and *Sailing to Byzantium*, the yearning for transformation, continuity, and return is palpable. The idea of the eternal soul moving through forms gave his poetry its unique blend of otherworldly beauty and earthly intensity.

Yeats's open embrace of reincarnation gave literary authority to the doctrine in the modern West. At a time when science and materialism dominated intellectual life, one of the era's most celebrated poets declared that he had lived before and would live again. His voice carried the weight of cultural legitimacy, making rebirth a theme fit not only for mystics but for Nobel laureates.

CARL JUNG (1875–1961)

BORN	KESSWIL, SWITZERLAND
DIED	KÜSNACHT, SWITZERLAND
PROFESSION	PSYCHOLOGIST; FOUNDER OF ANALYTICAL PSYCHOLOGY
KNOWN FOR	ARCHETYPES, COLLECTIVE UNCONSCIOUS, DREAM ANALYSIS

CARL GUSTAV JUNG, ONE OF THE MOST INFLUENTIAL PSYCHOLOGISTS of the 20th century, was fascinated by the symbolic patterns that shape human life. Unlike Freud, who reduced the psyche to sexuality and repression, Jung explored its mythic depths—dreams, visions, archetypes, and spiritual traditions. Inevitably, this exploration led him to the idea of reincarnation.

Jung regarded reincarnation not as dogma but as a compelling psychological hypothesis. He saw in it both an explanation for archetypal memories that surface in dreams and visions, and a cross-cultural truth that reappears in every major tradition. In his autobiographical *Memories, Dreams, Reflections*, he wrote:

> "Reincarnation is... a most probable hypothesis. It is not more extraordinary than the assumption that our life is a new one."
>
> — *MEMORIES, DREAMS, REFLECTIONS* (1962)

Privately, Jung sometimes spoke in even more personal terms, describing dreams in which he seemed to recall earlier existences. In one striking case, he told a colleague that he felt he had lived in the 18th century, even picturing himself in clothing of that period.

Yet as a scientist, Jung insisted on caution. He did not claim to prove rebirth but argued that the psyche itself behaves as though it is immortal—weaving myths, symbols, and intuitions that point beyond a single lifespan. His concept of the "collective unconscious" made space for reincarnation by framing it as part of humanity's archetypal inheritance.

Jung's authority as a psychiatrist gave reincarnation a place in modern intellectual life. By treating it as a serious hypothesis rather than a superstition, he opened the door for psychology to dialogue with religion, myth, and spiritual traditions. His legacy still inspires therapists, philosophers, and seekers who suspect that the human story is larger than one birth and one death.

ALDOUS HUXLEY (1894–1963)

BORN	GODALMING, SURREY, ENGLAND
DIED	LOS ANGELES, USA
PROFESSION	NOVELIST; ESSAYIST; PHILOSOPHER
KNOWN FOR	*BRAVE NEW WORLD; THE PERENNIAL PHILOSOPHY*

ALDOUS HUXLEY WAS ONE OF THE 20TH CENTURY'S GREAT intellectual explorers—a novelist, philosopher, and cultural critic who moved effortlessly between literature, science, and mysticism. Famous for his dystopian classic *Brave New World* (1932), he also became a leading interpreter of Eastern philosophy for Western audiences.

Huxley's spiritual masterpiece, *The Perennial Philosophy* (1945), gathered teachings from Hinduism, Buddhism, Christianity, Islam, and Taoism, seeking the timeless truths they shared. Among these, reincarnation stood out as the most rational explanation for both the moral order of the universe and the freedom of the individual.

> "The doctrine of rebirth is the only metaphysic which finds room for both divine justice and human freedom."
> — *THE PERENNIAL PHILOSOPHY* (1945)

For Huxley, reincarnation reconciled two essential truths: that the universe is just (no action is without consequence) and that humans are free (each life is a chance to choose anew). Without rebirth, he argued, either justice or freedom must be sacrificed.

His interest was not merely theoretical. Huxley's later years in California brought him into contact with Vedanta teachers, yoga, and psychedelics—all of which reinforced his conviction that consciousness survives bodily death. He believed that the soul's journey through multiple lives was part of the "perennial philosophy" shared by humanity's greatest sages.

Huxley died on 22 November 1963, the same day as John F. Kennedy and C.S. Lewis. On his deathbed, his wife Laura injected him with LSD at his request—a final attempt to enter the next life with expanded consciousness. His passing thus embodied the synthesis he sought: literature, philosophy, science, and mystical experiment joined in a search for continuity beyond death.

TIMOTHY LEARY (1920–1996)

BORN	SPRINGFIELD, MASSACHUSETTS, USA
DIED	BEVERLY HILLS, CALIFORNIA, USA
PROFESSION	PSYCHOLOGIST; WRITER; COUNTERCULTURE ICON
KNOWN FOR	HARVARD LSD RESEARCH; "TURN ON, TUNE IN, DROP OUT"

TIMOTHY LEARY BECAME ONE OF THE MOST CONTROVERSIAL FIGURES of the 1960s—a Harvard psychologist turned psychedelic prophet. Initially respected for his work on personality and psychotherapy, he became famous (and infamous) for his experiments with psilocybin and LSD, which he saw as tools for expanding consciousness. Forced out of Harvard, pursued by the U.S. government, and lionised by the counterculture, Leary turned himself into a symbol of rebellion against mainstream society.

For Leary, reincarnation was less a matter of metaphysics than of continual transformation. He spoke of the psychedelic journey as a form of death-and-rebirth, a rehearsal for the great transition that awaits all humans. In *The Psychedelic Experience* (1964), which he co-authored with Richard Alpert (later Ram Dass), he presented the Tibetan *Bardo Thödol* as a manual for navigating altered states:

> "A psychedelic experience is a journey to new realms of consciousness. *The Tibetan Book of the Dead* is the basic source book for understanding all psychedelic experiences."
>
> — *THE PSYCHEDELIC EXPERIENCE* (1964)

You Again

Later in life, Leary treated physical death itself as another chapter in this ongoing transformation:

> "Death is the last great adventure."
> — *Flashbacks* (1983)

In his reframing, reincarnation was not only about survival after death but about the endless potential for renewal of consciousness here and now. By linking Tibetan teachings with modern psychology, and by speaking of death as adventure rather than extinction, Leary carried the language of rebirth into the countercultural mainstream.

RAM DASS (1931–2019)

Born	Newton, Massachusetts, USA
Died	Maui, Hawaii, USA
Profession	Psychologist; spiritual teacher; author
Known For	*Be Here Now*; popularising Hindu philosophy in the West

Ram Dass, born Richard Alpert, began his career as a Harvard psychologist alongside Timothy Leary, pioneering research into psychedelics in the early 1960s. After his dismissal from Harvard and a turbulent period of experimentation, he travelled to India in 1967, where he met his guru, Neem Karoli Baba. This encounter transformed his life and gave birth to his spiritual persona, "Ram Dass" ("Servant of God").

Unlike Leary, who often treated reincarnation metaphorically, Ram Dass embraced it as a literal truth of Hindu philosophy. In his breakthrough book *Be Here Now* (1971), he presented the teaching with striking simplicity:

> "I am not this body. I am not this role. I am a soul. As such, I have lived thousands of lives and will live thousands more until I am free."
>
> — *Be Here Now* (1971)

For him, reincarnation was not an abstract doctrine but a practical perspective: life's trials made sense when seen as part of a long journey of the soul. Death, far from being an end, was simply another transition in the ongoing curriculum of existence.

He also used reincarnation to soften the fear of death for Western audiences. In his later book *Still Here* (2000), written after a stroke left him partially paralysed, he reflected:

> "Death is absolutely safe. It's like taking off a tight shoe."
> — *Still Here* (2000)

Through his writings, lectures, and retreats, Ram Dass introduced countless seekers to *karma* and rebirth, translating Indian philosophy into accessible, compassionate language. His authority as a Harvard-trained psychologist gave his testimony special weight: reincarnation was not superstition, he insisted, but part of the soul's evolution toward freedom.

OF THE WISE & GLORIOUS

ARTISTS, WRITERS & MUSICIANS

FROM ZHUANGZI'S PLAYFULNESS IN ANCIENT CHINA TO RAM DASS's gentle guidance in modern America, these philosophers, mystics, and seekers testify to a remarkable continuity: the idea of rebirth has never belonged to one age or culture alone. Each voice framed it in a different idiom—mathematics for Pythagoras, poetry for Virgil and Wordsworth, philosophy for Plato and Schopenhauer, psychology for Jung, and spiritual teaching for Ram Dass—yet all converged on the same conviction that life flows on beyond a single span.

Their testimony shows that reincarnation has appealed not only to mystics and visionaries but also to some of the most rational, creative, and disciplined minds of history. It is not an eccentric belief on the margins, but a current running through the heart of philosophy itself.

YOU AGAIN

The chorus only grows louder when we turn from philosophers to artists and musicians—figures who shaped culture not through abstract reasoning but through song, image, and performance. In them, the doctrine of rebirth found new life, reaching millions through art and popular imagination.

GEORGE HARRISON (1943–2001)

Born	Liverpool, England
Died	Los Angeles, USA
Profession	Musician; guitarist for The Beatles
Known for	*My Sweet Lord*; pioneering Indian music in in Western rock; Hare Krishna devotion

George Harrison, the "quiet Beatle," became the most spiritually engaged member of the world's most famous band. His encounter with Indian sitar master Ravi Shankar in the mid-1960s opened the door to Hindu philosophy, meditation, and the Hare Krishna movement, which shaped the rest of his life and music.

Unlike many Western celebrities dabbling in Eastern mysticism, Harrison lived the path sincerely. He chanted daily, supported the International Society for Krishna Consciousness (ISKCON), and openly spoke of *karma* and reincarnation as guiding principles. In interviews, he was blunt:

> "If you don't look after yourself,
> then you have to come back and try again until you do."
> — *Rolling Stone interview*, 1979

For Harrison, reincarnation was not a vague speculation but a practical truth. It explained why ethical living mattered, why the soul must cultivate love of God, and why death should not be feared. His solo work—most famously the song *My Sweet Lord* (1970)—carried these convictions into popular culture, blending rock music with explicit *bhakti* devotion.

Through Harrison, millions of fans encountered Indian philosophy for the first time. His life demonstrated that even at the heights of fame, the search for meaning pointed beyond one lifetime. In his words and music, rebirth became part of the soundtrack of the modern West.

Of the Wise & Glorious

DAVID BOWIE (1947–2016)

BORN	LONDON, ENGLAND
DIED	NEW YORK CITY, USA
PROFESSION	MUSICIAN; ACTOR; ARTIST
KNOWN FOR	ZIGGY STARDUST; *HEROES*; CONSTANT REINVENTION

DAVID BOWIE, one of the most innovative musicians of the 20th century, built his career on transformation—changing personas as fluidly as others change clothes. Behind this artistic shape-shifting lay a deep fascination with spirituality, particularly Tibetan Buddhism and reincarnation.

In the late 1960s, before he became a global icon, Bowie studied Tibetan teachings and seriously considered becoming a Buddhist monk. His interest in rebirth was not a passing curiosity. In a 1967 interview with *Melody Maker*, the young musician declared:

> "My interest in Buddhism is infinite.
> The only thing I'm certain of is reincarnation."
> — *MELODY MAKER*, 1967

This conviction echoed throughout his art. His stage personas—from Ziggy Stardust to the Thin White Duke—can be read as theatrical reincarnations, each death onstage paving the way for a new life. His lifelong fascination with mortality, change, and renewal gave his work an intensity that resonated with audiences across generations.

Though Bowie never committed to a single religious path, reincarnation remained one of the few metaphysical ideas he affirmed with confidence. For him, it was not merely doctrine but a metaphor for creativity itself: identity is fluid, self is provisional, and transformation is the law of life.

By bringing such ideas into the world of popular culture, Bowie helped normalise reincarnation for a global audience. His testimony shows that even at the heights of modern celebrity, the ancient belief in rebirth continued to inspire—both in philosophy and in art.

SHIRLEY MACLAINE (B. 1934)

BORN RICHMOND, VIRGINIA, USA

PROFESSION ACTRESS; AUTHOR

KNOWN FOR ACADEMY AWARD-WINNING ACTING CAREER; SPIRITUAL AUTOBIOGRAPHIES

Shirley MacLaine, one of Hollywood's most celebrated actresses, became equally famous for her outspoken embrace of reincarnation. At the height of her career in the 1980s, she startled mainstream audiences by publishing a series of autobiographical books—beginning with *Out on a Limb* (1983)—in which she recounted vivid past-life memories, out-of-body experiences, and her conviction that the soul journeys through countless lifetimes.

Her candour helped bring the doctrine of rebirth from esoteric circles into living rooms across America. Millions of readers, many encountering the idea for the first time, were introduced to *karma* and reincarnation through her personal testimony. She was unflinching about her certainty:

> "I knew I had lived before. I knew I would live again."
> — *OUT ON A LIMB* (1983)

MacLaine's spiritual writings—which went on to include *Dancing in the Light* (1985) and *The Camino* (2000)—made her one of the most visible Western voices for reincarnation. Her work sparked public debates, television specials, and even satire, yet she never wavered. For her, rebirth was not an exotic theory but an experiential truth discovered through inner exploration.

By sharing her beliefs so openly, MacLaine helped shift reincarnation into mainstream Western culture. What had been seen as an eccentric or marginal idea became part of popular conversation, shaping the spiritual outlook of millions.

Scientists, Physicians & Psychologists

From poets and performers to philosophers and mystics, reincarnation has spoken to the imagination of humanity in every age. Artists gave it melody and image; musicians and actors carried it into popular culture. But the chorus of voices does not end with the arts. Even those committed to the rigour of science and medicine—astronomers, inventors, physicians, and psychologists—found reason to take the idea seriously. For them, rebirth was not only a myth or metaphor, but a hypothesis about the continuity of consciousness and the moral order of the universe.

You Again

CAMILLE FLAMMARION (1842–1925)

Born	Montigny-le-Roi, France
Died	Juvisy-sur-Orge, France
Profession	Astronomer; author
Known For	Popular astronomy; *Death and Its Mystery*; early science writing on life after death

Nicolas Camille Flammarion was a French astronomer and author who combined rigorous science with a passionate curiosity about the soul. A student of Urbain Le Verrier at the Paris Observatory, he later founded his own observatory at Juvisy. While he made legitimate contributions to astronomy—cataloguing double stars and writing important works on the atmosphere of Mars—he is best remembered for his prolific books that made the cosmos accessible to the general public.

Flammarion believed that science and spirituality need not be opposed. In works like *Lumen* (1867) and *Death and Its Mystery* (1920–21), he explored the survival of consciousness after death and argued in favour of reincarnation. He presented himself as a modern Pythagorean, convinced that astronomical discovery and the doctrine of rebirth were compatible:

> "Let us be Pythagoreans who have reappeared in the twentieth century… present scientific methods have brought practical confirmation."
>
> — *Death and Its Mystery* (1920s)

Flammarion's writings placed reincarnation squarely within the conversation of modern science. He was a member of the SOCIETY FOR PSYCHICAL RESEARCH and corresponded with scientists across Europe about evidence for the persistence of consciousness. His blend of astronomy and metaphysics made him a bridge figure between scientific rationalism and spiritual speculation.

To the public, he offered a vision of the universe alive with meaning: stars were not merely burning gas but symbols of endless renewal, and souls, like celestial bodies, moved in eternal cycles. By affirming reincarnation as scientifically plausible, Flammarion gave the doctrine credibility in an age otherwise dominated by materialism.

OF THE WISE & GLORIOUS

THOMAS EDISON (1847–1931)

BORN	MILAN, OHIO, USA
DIED	WEST ORANGE, NEW JERSEY, USA
PROFESSION	INVENTOR
KNOWN FOR	LIGHT BULB; PHONOGRAPH; MOTION PICTURES; OVER 1,000 PATENTS

THOMAS ALVA EDISON, THE "WIZARD OF MENLO PARK," WAS THE most prolific inventor of modern times. His creations—the phonograph, electric light bulb, and motion picture camera—transformed daily life. A self-taught genius with little formal education, he embodied the practical spirit of American ingenuity.

Yet even Edison, the great material inventor, speculated about the persistence of consciousness and cycles of return. In interviews from the 1910s, he suggested that life might not end with death but continue in new earthly cycles.

In a *New York Times* interview, he remarked:

> "The only survival I can conceive is to start a new Earth cycle again."
>
> — *NEW YORK TIMES*, C. 1910S

Edison also toyed with the idea of building a device to communicate with the dead—not in a mystical sense, but as an experiment in physics. Though he never produced such an invention, his willingness to speak publicly about survival and new beginnings shows that reincarnation was not unthinkable even to the most pragmatic of minds.

For Edison, rebirth was not a religious doctrine but a scientific possibility, an extension of the law of conservation: energy is never destroyed, only transformed. His voice illustrates that the idea of life's return could find resonance even in the workshop of modern technology.

HENRY FORD (1863–1947)

BORN	GREENFIELD TOWNSHIP, MICHIGAN, USA
DIED	DEARBORN, MICHIGAN, USA
PROFESSION	INDUSTRIALIST; FOUNDER OF FORD MOTOR COMPANY
KNOWN FOR	REVOLUTIONISING INDUSTRY WITH THE MOVING ASSEMBLY LINE; MODEL T AUTOMOBILE

HENRY FORD, ONE OF THE MOST INFLUENTIAL INDUSTRIALISTS OF the 20th century, transformed modern life by making automobiles affordable for ordinary people. His assembly line methods reshaped global industry, creating both admiration and controversy. Behind his reputation as a hard-headed businessman, however, Ford also held unconventional spiritual beliefs—among them, reincarnation.

In a 1928 interview with the *San Francisco Examiner*, Ford explained that he had adopted the doctrine as a young man:

> "I adopted the theory of reincarnation when I was twenty-six. ... When I discovered reincarnation, it was as if I had found a universal plan. I realised that there was a chance to work out my ideas. Time was no longer limited... I no longer feared death."
> — *SAN FRANCISCO EXAMINER*, 1928

For Ford, reincarnation offered freedom from anxiety and a sense of limitless opportunity. It provided a framework in which mistakes could be corrected and unfinished projects resumed in future lives. Just as his factories recycled materials and reshaped them into new forms, so he imagined the soul moving from one body to another.

That one of the most practical men of modern history embraced reincarnation gave the doctrine unusual credibility. Ford's testimony shows that rebirth could appeal not only to mystics and philosophers, but also to those who lived and thrived in the world of machines and industry.

W. C. ALVAREZ, M.D. (1884–1978)

BORN	SAN FRANCISCO, USA
DIED	BERKELEY, CALIFORNIA, USA
PROFESSION	PHYSICIAN; MEDICAL WRITER
KNOWN FOR	*NERVES IN COLLISION*; MEDICAL COLUMNS; MAYO CLINIC AFFILIATION

WALTER CLEMENT ALVAREZ WAS AN AMERICAN PHYSICIAN AND prolific medical writer who spent much of his career at the Mayo Clinic. He specialised in gastroenterology but became best known for his clear, accessible medical advice in books and newspaper columns read by millions.

Unusually for a doctor of his standing, Alvarez spoke openly about his personal belief in reincarnation. In a 1952 interview with the *Los Angeles Times,* he made a candid remark about carrying his temperament into another life:

> "If I am to have another incarnation, I'll take those nerves again, rather than my father's placid, less bothersome ones."
>
> — *LOS ANGELES TIMES*, 1952

His words were half-humorous but unmistakably sincere, showing that he regarded rebirth as a real possibility. By voicing such views in mainstream media, Alvarez brought the subject of reincarnation into modern medical conversation.

Though not a mystic or philosopher, Alvarez represents a striking category: a conventional Western physician who nonetheless found reincarnation the best explanation for temperament and character. His public testimony helped normalise the doctrine, making it part of mid-20th-century popular discourse on health, heredity, and personality.

ALBERT SCHWEITZER (1875–1965)

BORN	KAYSERSBERG, ALSACE (THEN GERMANY)
DIED	LAMBARÉNÉ, GABON
PROFESSION	PHYSICIAN; THEOLOGIAN, HUMANITARIAN; NOBEL LAUREATE
KNOWN FOR	MISSIONARY HOSPITAL IN AFRICA; ETHIC OF "REVERENCE FOR LIFE"; NOBEL PEACE PRIZE (1952)

ALBERT SCHWEITZER WAS ONE OF THE 20TH CENTURY'S MOST admired humanitarians. A theologian, philosopher, organist, and physician, he abandoned an academic career in Europe to build and run a hospital in Lambaréné, Gabon, where he served for decades. His ethic of *Ehrfurcht vor dem Leben* ("Reverence for Life") earned him global acclaim and the 1952 Nobel Peace Prize.

At the heart of this ethic lay his conviction in rebirth. Schweitzer described reincarnation as one of the greatest truths he had discovered, a principle that deepened his compassion for all living beings:

> "I was compelled to recognise and confess the idea of rebirth as one of the greatest of truths."
> — *ON THE EDGE OF THE PRIMEVAL FOREST* (1922)

For Schweitzer, reincarnation meant that life is continuous, that every creature participates in the same great cycle, and that harming others ultimately harms oneself. This belief underpinned his radical commitment to nonviolence, animal welfare, and the sanctity of all forms of life.

His testimony carried unusual weight. Here was not a mystic or poet, but a Nobel Prize–winning physician and theologian—a man whose credibility rested on both scientific skill and moral authority. By affirming reincarnation as integral to his worldview, Schweitzer offered Western audiences a vision in which compassion, ethics, and the continuity of the soul formed one seamless whole.

NOTICE.

These interpretations remain *controversial* within mainstream science, and readers are encouraged to explore the literature and form their own views. In these studies, the term 'evidence' is used in the sense the researchers themselves define—not in the strict biomedical sense of controlled experiment.

IAN STEVENSON, M.D. (1918–2007)

BORN	MONTREAL, CANADA
DIED	CHARLOTTESVILLE, VIRGINIA, USA
PROFESSION	PSYCHIATRIST
KNOWN FOR	*TWENTY CASES SUGGESTIVE OF REINCARNATION*; PIONEERING PAST-LIFE CASE STUDIES

IAN STEVENSON, LONGTIME CHAIR OF PSYCHIATRY AT THE UNIVERSITY of Virginia, devoted his career to a subject most of his peers avoided: children's memories of previous lives. Beginning in the 1960s, he travelled to India, Sri Lanka, Lebanon, Alaska, and beyond, compiling thousands of case reports. He paid special attention to children who spontaneously recalled details of a past life—names, places, deaths—that could later be verified. Often he documented physical birthmarks or deformities that corresponded to the wounds or injuries of the deceased person the child claimed to have been.

Stevenson was cautious by temperament. He never claimed to "prove" reincarnation, but his monumental works—including *Twenty Cases Suggestive of Reincarnation* (1966) and the multi-volume *Cases of the Reincarnation Type* (1975–83)—established a new field of empirical research into survival and memory. His meticulous cross-checking, interviews with families, and statistical analyses raised the debate above hearsay. As the *New York Times* obituary noted, Stevenson "piled up case after case that defied easy dismissal."

His conclusions were understated but clear: in the strongest cases, reincarnation remained the most compelling hypothesis. His willingness to treat rebirth not as superstition but as a scientific question gave the idea unprecedented credibility in modern psychiatry.

> "Of the cases we now know, reincarnation—at least for some—is the best explanation we have been able to come up with."
> — *Twenty Cases Suggestive of Reincarnation* (1974)

Stevenson's work laid the foundation for a new generation of researchers, including his colleagues Jim B. Tucker and Erlendur Haraldsson, ensuring that serious discussion of reincarnation would remain within the boundaries of academic psychology.

BRIAN WEISS (B. 1944)

BORN	NEW YORK, USA
PROFESSION	PSYCHIATRIST, AUTHOR
KNOWN FOR	*MANY LIVES, MANY MASTERS*; PAST-LIFE REGRESSION THERAPY

BRIAN WEISS TRAINED IN THE MOST CONVENTIONAL OF SETTINGS—Columbia University, Yale Medical School, and a residency in psychiatry at Yale. He became Chief of Psychiatry at Mount Sinai Medical Centre in Miami, specialising in anxiety disorders and depression. Yet his career took an extraordinary turn in the early 1980s when a patient under hypnosis began recalling what seemed to be past lives.

Weiss was initially sceptical. But as the patient described verifiable details and reported transformative healing from chronic fears, he was compelled to reconsider. The result was his best-selling *Many Lives, Many Masters* (1988), which brought reincarnation into mainstream psychotherapy. He went on to write further works—*Through Time into Healing* (1992), *Same Soul, Many Bodies* (2004)—and to conduct seminars worldwide.

Weiss's influence has been cultural as much as clinical, while critics dismissed his work as anecdotal, millions of readers encountered the possibility of reincarnation through his patient stories. His case material suggested that trauma, phobias, and even physical symptoms could be traced to experiences in former lives—and that healing often came when these memories were integrated.

> "For truly we are all immortal. Our bodies are the shells, the garments of the soul."
> — *Many Lives, Many Masters* (1988)

By reframing reincarnation not as mysticism but as a tool for healing, Weiss opened a door for countless Westerners to take the idea seriously.

JIM B. TUCKER M.D. (B. 1960)

BORN	NORTH CAROLINA, USA
PROFESSION	PSYCHIATRIST; RESEARCHER
KNOWN FOR	DIRECTOR OF THE DIVISION OF PERCEPTUAL STUDIES AT THE UNIVERSITY OF VIRGINIA; CONTINUATION OF STEVENSON'S WORK ON CHILDREN'S PAST-LIFE

JIM TUCKER, A CHILD PSYCHIATRIST BY TRAINING, STEPPED INTO THE shoes of Ian Stevenson at the University of Virginia's Division of Perceptual Studies. Where Stevenson had pioneered the fieldwork, Tucker brought a new statistical rigour and a North American focus.

His books *Life Before Life* (2005) and *Return to Life* (2013) presented detailed American cases of children who spontaneously spoke of previous lives—often with names, places, and circumstances later verified. One famous subject, James Leininger, described in detail the life of a World War II fighter pilot, knowledge his family insisted he could not have acquired normally.

Tucker's contribution has been to frame reincarnation research in language palatable to both scientists and the public. He conducted large-scale surveys, used probability analyses, and published in peer-reviewed journals. Unlike Weiss, he avoided therapeutic regression techniques, focusing only on spontaneous cases in children—those least contaminated by suggestion or cultural expectation.

> "The evidence in these cases is quite strong... the best explanation is that memories, emotions, and even physical injuries can carry over from one life to the next."
> — *Return to Life* (2013)

Tucker's willingness to state plainly that reincarnation is the "best explanation" marks one of the rare moments where mainstream medical science has leaned toward affirming rebirth.

ERLENDUR HARALDSSON (1931–2020)

Born	Reykjavík, Iceland
Died	Reykjavík, Iceland
Profession	Psychologist; professor of psychology; University of Iceland
Known For	Cross-cultural studies of children with past-life memories; research into deathbed visions, apparitions, and survival of consciousness

Erlendur Haraldsson was a pioneering figure bridging rigorous psychology with fringe phenomena. Educated in Iceland, Edinburgh, Freiburg, and Munich, he became a professor at the University of Iceland, and over many decades conducted field research in Sri Lanka, Lebanon, Iceland, and elsewhere. He collaborated with Ian Stevenson in the 1970s and later authored *I Saw a Light and Came Here: Children's Experiences of Reincarnation*. His work covered not only children's claimed past-life memories but also deathbed visions, apparitions, and the psychology of belief.

Haraldsson's studies of children revealed consistent patterns: many begin speaking of a past life at about two to three years old; many recall details of how a past personality died—often violently—and sometimes show phobias that correlate with those circumstances. He found that these children perform as well or better in certain verbal and memory tasks than their peers, but do not show greater suggestibility in most tests.

> "We gathered a lot of cases in the United States from American doctors and nurses. Then we also wanted to do

> it in others countries with a different religion and a different culture. So it was also conducted in India. There we visited many university hospitals… who have witnessed many patients having visions of people who have passed away."
>
> — ERLENDUR HARALDSSON IN *STORIES OF REINCARNATION: MANY ROADS*

Haraldsson was careful about making claims: his conclusions were modest, yet he argued such evidence demands attention. For him, these phenomena aren't proof in the scientific-sense, but they are phenomena that challenge conventional explanations. His work helped to show that past-life memory reports and related experiences occur globally and that in a number of cases verification of details is successful.

SATWANT K. PASRICHA (B. *circa.* 1945)

BORN	INDIA
PROFESSION	CLINICAL PSYCHOLOGIST, RESEARCHER
KNOWN FOR	PROFESSOR OF PSYCHOLOGY AT NIMHANS, BANGALORE; COLLABORATOR WITH IAN STEVENSON; LEADING INDIAN RESEARCHER OF PAST-LIFE MEMORY CASES

SATWANT PASRICHA IS ONE OF THE FOREMOST INDIAN PSYCHOLOGISTS to have systematically studied reincarnation. Trained at the National Institute of Mental Health and Neurosciences (NIMHANS) in Bangalore—India's premier psychiatric research centre—she combined clinical psychology with extensive fieldwork in rural communities. Beginning in the 1970s, she collaborated with Ian Stevenson, documenting dozens of cases in which children reported detailed memories of earlier lives.

Her research paid special attention to India's cultural context. Whereas Western critics sometimes argued that past-life memories were products of suggestion, Pasricha showed that children often spoke out spontaneously at very young ages, in families that did not encourage such claims. She carefully cross-checked statements, family histories, and circumstances of the alleged previous life, adding an Indian perspective that complemented Stevenson's international cases.

Pasricha also published widely in Indian and international journals, bringing reincarnation research into professional discourse. She emphasised that the best cases included verifiable statements, recognisable birthmarks, and behavioural continuities that could not easily be explained by chance, fraud, or cultural conditioning.

> "The best interpretation of these cases is that they provide evidence of reincarnation."
> — *Journal of Scientific Exploration* (1990s)

Her role as a senior academic in India gave the study unusual legitimacy. In a society where rebirth is taken for granted culturally, her insistence on rigorous documentation helped separate folklore from genuine scientific investigation. Through her work, the study of reincarnation became not just a matter of belief, but a field of empirical research grounded in psychology.

Religious Leaders & Mystics

From physicians and psychiatrists to psychologists and inventors, modern science has not been immune to the pull of rebirth. Some approached it with humour, others with statistical rigour, still others with stories from their clinics and research fields. The chorus of testimony is striking: even within the halls of medicine and laboratories of science, reincarnation has remained the "best explanation" for certain otherwise inexplicable cases. Yet science is not the only domain where the doctrine has been taken seriously. For millennia, spiritual teachers, mystics, and religious reformers have affirmed that the soul returns again and again—not merely as hypothesis, but as lived conviction. It is to these voices of faith and vision that we now turn.

You Again

OF THE WISE & GLORIOUS

KAMO NO CHŌMEI (1153–1216)

BORN   KYOTO, JAPAN
DIED   HINO, JAPAN
PROFESSION   POET; ESSAYIST; BUDDHIST RECLUSE
KNOWN FOR   *HŌJŌKI* (AN ACCOUNT OF MY HUT)

KAMO NO CHŌMEI STANDS AT THE THRESHOLD BETWEEN COURTLY refinement and monastic withdrawal—a poet who saw the vanity of worldly achievement and turned his insight into literature of timeless simplicity. Born into a Shinto priestly family in Kyoto, he was trained in the court's elegant arts of poetry and music. For years he sought official recognition, yet his ambitions were thwarted by politics and rank. Then, as if mirroring his inner disillusionment, the capital itself seemed to disintegrate. Earthquakes, fires, famine, and plague devastated Kyoto in his lifetime; entire districts vanished overnight.

These calamities shaped the lens through which Chōmei viewed existence. Around the age of fifty, he renounced the city and withdrew first to the hills of Ohara and later to a hermitage in Hino, south of Kyoto. There he lived in a hut barely ten feet square—a deliberate miniature of the impermanent world—and wrote *Hōjōki* ("An Account of My Hut"), one of the cornerstones of Japanese introspective prose.

The work opens with a vision of ceaseless change: "The flow of the river never ceases, and the water that passes is never the same." From this image unfolds a meditation on impermanence (*mujō*), the doctrine that all compounded things arise and perish. For Chōmei, human life, like the river's current, offers no fixed foothold. Yet within this flux lies a serene acceptance: to recognise transience is to glimpse liberation.

His reflections echo the Buddhist conviction that existence unfolds through countless transformations. Though Chōmei does not theorise rebirth explicitly, his language of drifting from form to form carries the unmistakable rhythm of *saṃsāra*—the current that bears every being through cycles of birth and dissolution. His small hut becomes a microcosm of that vast process: fragile, temporary, yet sufficient for awakening.

In the stillness of solitude, Chōmei found what his courtly life could not offer—direct awareness of the endless arising and passing of all things. His life and writing became a parable for spiritual detachment: that freedom is not escape from the world, but a clear seeing of its impermanence.

> "I have drifted through many lives, as one who floats on the current, carried from one existence to another."
> — *HŌJŌKI* (EARLY 13TH CENTURY)

RAMAKRISHNA PARAMAHAMSA (1836–1886)

Born	Kamarpukur, Bengal, India
Died	Cossipore, Calcutta, India
Profession	Mystic; Hindu saint
Known For	Devotional mysticism; influence on Vivekananda

Ramakrishna Paramahamsa stands as one of the purest voices of India's spiritual renaissance—a mystic whose life became a living synthesis of the world's religions. Born in a poor but devout Brahmin family in rural Bengal, he was drawn from childhood to ecstatic states of worship. As a young man he became the temple priest at Dakshineswar, near Calcutta, where his unguarded devotion to the goddess Kālī soon deepened into trance and revelation.

Those who met him saw not a theologian but a man consumed by direct experience of the Divine. He would pass from rapture to tears, from laughter to stillness, describing visions of the Mother as one might describe encounters with sunlight. Over years of practice, he experimented with every major religious path available to him—Tantric, Vaiṣṇava, Islamic, and Christian—and in each he claimed to realise the same eternal Reality. For Ramakrishna, truth was one; the forms through which it manifests are many.

Reincarnation, for him, was not an abstract philosophy but the natural expression of this divine unity. Souls, he said, return again and again, not as punishment but as education, learning through joy and sorrow until they awaken to the Divine within. "The bound soul may go to different worlds after death," he taught, "and may be born again and again; only when it realises GOD does it escape the wheel of birth and death." In his view, liberation (*mokṣa*) was not earned through austerity alone but through love—the surrender of the separate self into the infinite compassion of GOD.

His disciples included Narendranath Dutta, later known as Swami Vivekānanda, who would carry these teachings to the West and ignite the first global interest in yoga and *Vedanta*. Through him, Ramakrishna's living testimony reached millions: the conviction that divinity lies in every heart, and that through devotion, service, and meditation one can awaken to it here and now.

In his final years, ravaged by throat cancer yet serene, he told his followers that he would return "again and again" for the good of humanity—a promise that made reincarnation not a doctrine to debate but a vow of compassion. His life remains a luminous bridge between the mystical and the universal, showing that the soul's journey across lifetimes is nothing less than the unfolding of divine love itself.

> "The bound soul may go to different worlds after death, may be born again and again. Only when it realises GOD does it escape the wheel of birth and death."
>
> — *SAYINGS OF RAMAKRISHNA*

HELENA BLAVATSKY (1831–1891)

BORN	YEKATERINOSLAV, RUSSIA
DIED	LONDON, ENGLAND
PROFESSION	OCCULTIST; WRITER; CO-FOUNDER OF THE THEOSOPHICAL SOCIETY
KNOWN FOR	*THE SECRET DOCTRINE*; *THE KEY TO THEOSOPHY*; INTRODUCING EASTERN PHILOSOPHY TO THE MODERN WEST

HELENA PETROVNA BLAVATSKY WAS ONE OF THE MOST influential—and controversial—spiritual figures of the modern era. A restless traveller, polyglot, and seeker of hidden knowledge, she moved through a 19th-century world awakening to science yet hungry for meaning. Her life spanned continents: from Russia to Egypt, from Tibet (by her own account) to America and England. In 1875, with Colonel Henry Steel Olcott, she founded the THEOSOPHICAL SOCIETY IN NEW YORK —an organisation dedicated to the comparative study of religion, philosophy, and science, and to the cultivation of a universal brotherhood transcending creed or race.

Through her monumental writings *Isis Unveiled* (1877) and *The Secret Doctrine* (1888), Blavatsky became the principal architect of Western esotericism's modern revival. She proposed that all religions share a single ancient source—the "Wisdom-Tradition"—guarded for ages by adepts in the East. Among its central teachings was reincarnation, not as mystical fancy but as a natural law woven into the evolution of consciousness. "Reincarnation," she wrote, "is the law of life; it explains the inequalities of birth and fortune, of intellect and capacities." Every soul, she taught, is a pilgrim on an immense journey through matter and spirit, gathering experience until it attains mastery and compassion.

Her presentation of *karma* and rebirth was radical for Victorian readers. She framed them not as superstition but as a scientific necessity within a moral universe: nothing is lost, every cause yields its effect, and the soul, like energy, is indestructible. Her blend of mysticism, science, and moral law offered a new metaphysics for an age of disillusionment—a bridge between faith and reason.

Blavatsky's legacy is vast. She inspired the birth of modern comparative religion, influenced artists from Kandinsky to Yeats, and seeded later movements from the New Age to esoteric Buddhism. Detractors accused her of fabrication; admirers saw her as a channel for forgotten truths. Whatever one's verdict, her impact is undeniable: she re-introduced the West to the ancient idea that the human spirit evolves through countless lives toward unity with the divine.

> "Reincarnation is the law of life... It explains the inequalities of birth and fortune, of intellect and capacities."
>
> — *THE KEY TO THEOSOPHY* (1889)

ANNIE BESANT (1847–1933)

Born	London, England
Died	Adyar, India
Profession	Social reformer; activist; Theosophist
Known For	Presidency of the Theosophical Society; writings on karma and reincarnation

Annie Besant lived two extraordinary lives in one. In her early years she was a fierce social reformer: campaigning for women's rights, workers' rights, secular education, and birth control in Victorian England. Later, she turned to Theosophy, the esoteric movement that sought to unite Eastern wisdom with Western spirituality. Rising to lead the Theosophical Society, she became one of the most visible and articulate Western voices for *karma* and reincarnation in the early twentieth century.

For Besant, reincarnation was not an exotic theory but a law of moral development. The soul, she taught, returns again and again in progressively more capable forms, unfolding its faculties like a student climbing the rungs of education. Each life was another lesson in the soul's long school. *Karma* was the teacher: ensuring that no act, good or bad, was ever wasted, but always carried forward until mastered.

Her insistence that reincarnation was both rational and ethical helped make the doctrine respectable in modern Western culture, linking it with ideas of progress and human perfectibility.

"In the light of reincarnation life changes its aspect, for it becomes the school of the eternal Man within us, who seeks therein his development, the Man that was and is and shall be, for whom the hour will never strike."

— ANNIE BESANT

SRI AUROBINDO (1872–1950)

BORN	CALCUTTA, INDIA
DIED	PONDICHERRY, INDIA
PROFESSION	PHILOSOPHER; YOGI; SPIRITUAL TEACHER
KNOWN FOR	FOUNDING *INTEGRAL YOGA*; AUROBINDO *ASHRAM*

& THE MOTHER (MIRRA ALFASSA, 1878–1973)

BORN	PARIS, FRANCE
DIED	PONDICHERRY, INDIA
PROFESSION	MYSTIC AND COLLABORATOR
KNOWN FOR	AUROBINDO *ASHRAM*

S**RI AUROBINDO** WAS A REVOLUTIONARY NATIONALIST BEFORE HE became a revolutionary philosopher. After leaving politics, he dedicated his life to developing *Integral Yoga*—a vision of human evolution in which consciousness itself is destined to rise and transform. By his side was Mirra Alfassa—known simply as **THE MOTHER**—who guided their community and expanded his teaching into a living practice. Together they founded the Aurobindo *Ashram* in Pondicherry, which became a centre of spiritual experiment.

Reincarnation, for them, was not punishment but progression. The outer personality—the habits, memories, and circumstances of each birth—dissolves at death. But the psychic being, the deep inner soul, continues across lives, carrying the essence of experience forward. Each rebirth is a step in a vast cosmic evolution, leading not only the individual but humanity itself toward a divine future.

Aurobindo spoke of life as a recurring rhythm, yet always advancing; The Mother clarified that what truly endures is the inner consciousness, "living throughout the ages and manifesting in a multitude of forms." Their vision framed reincarnation as a hopeful process: each life is both an opportunity and a responsibility in the long unfolding of spirit.

> "In rebirth it is not the external being... that is born again: it is only the psychic being that passes from body to body... If we go a little way within ourselves, we shall discover that there is in each of us a consciousness that has been living throughout the ages and manifesting in a multitude of forms."
>
> — THE MOTHER

PARAMAHANSA YOGANANDA (1893–1952)

BORN	GORAKHPUR, UTTAR PRADESH,
DIED	LOS ANGELES, USA
PROFESSION	SPIRITUAL TEACHER; YOGI; AUTHOR
KNOWN FOR	*AUTOBIOGRAPHY OF A YOGI*; FOUNDING THE SELF-REALIZATION FELLOWSHIP; INTRODUCING YOGA AND MEDITATION TO THE WEST

PARAMAHANSA YOGANANDA WAS THE FIRST GREAT YOGI OF MODERN India to make a permanent home in the West, translating the ancient science of self-realisation into the idiom of a new century. Born Mukunda Lal Ghosh into a devout Bengali family, he showed mystical inclinations from childhood, meditating for hours and seeking out saints in the Himalayan foothills. Trained by his guru, Swami Sri Yukteśwar he was charged with a single mission: to bring *Kriya Yoga*—the "airplane route to GOD," as he called it—to the wider world.

Arriving in America in 1920 to address a religious congress in Boston, Yogananda astonished audiences unused to the serenity and authority of a young Indian monk. His charisma and clarity made Eastern spirituality suddenly accessible to Western minds. He later founded the Self-Realisation Fellowship in Los Angeles, creating a network of temples and meditation centres that continues today.

His *Autobiography of a Yogi* (1946) became one of the most influential spiritual books of the twentieth century—a text that revealed to millions a vision of the universe charged with consciousness. Within it, reincarnation appears not as speculation but as the very grammar of divine evolution. "The soul," he wrote, "after leaving one body at death, enters another form according to its karmic impulses." For Yogananda, each lifetime is a chapter in the soul's unfolding education: joy and sorrow alike are lessons through which GOD teaches Himself in miniature.

He reconciled modern rationality with ancient metaphysics, describing *karma* and rebirth as expressions of the same law that governs energy and matter—conservation and transformation on a cosmic scale. Liberation (*mokṣa*) was not a reward for saints but a birthright for all who learn to master thought, breath, and desire. His gentle humour and democratic spirit brought India's timeless teachings to Hollywood stars and ordinary workers alike, reminding both that "the soul's adventure continues until perfection is attained."

Yogananda's passing was as remarkable as his life. In 1952, moments after delivering a speech praising India and America as partners in spiritual destiny, he collapsed and died—a serene smile on his face. Witnesses later reported that his body showed no decay for weeks, a phenomenon his followers took as proof of his mastery over matter. Whether miracle or mystery, it seemed a fitting farewell from a teacher who had spent his life showing that spirit and body, death and rebirth, are but changing garments of the one eternal Self.

> "The soul, after leaving one body at death,
> enters another form according to its karmic impulses."
> — *AUTOBIOGRAPHY OF A YOGI* (1946)

THE 14TH DALAI LAMA (B. 1935)

BORN TAKTSER, AMDO, TIBET

PROFESSION SPIRITUAL LEADER OF TIBETAN BUDDHISM

KNOWN FOR NOBEL PEACE PRIZE; SYMBOL OF TIBETAN EXILE AND COMPASSION; GLOBAL ADVOCATE FOR NONVIOLENCE AND INTERFAITH DIALOGUE

TENZIN GYATSO, THE 14TH DALAI LAMA, IS AMONG THE MOST WIDELY revered spiritual figures of the modern world—a living embodiment of the Buddhist principle that compassion endures beyond the bounds of one lifetime. According to Tibetan tradition, each Dalai Lama is a *tulku*, or recognised reincarnation, of his predecessor—a continuous stream of consciousness reborn to guide others on the path of liberation.

Born Lhamo Dhondup in a small village in *Amdo*, he was identified at the age of two through a series of visions, divinations, and tests as the rebirth of the 13th Dalai Lama. Enthroned in Lhasa in 1940, his childhood was spent in rigorous study of Buddhist philosophy, logic, and meditation, preparing him not only for spiritual leadership but for a life of profound trial. When Chinese forces occupied Tibet in 1950, he was thrust into political responsibility at the age of fifteen. A decade later, after a failed uprising, he fled across the Himalayas into India, where he has lived in exile ever since.

From his new home in *Dharamsala*, the Dalai Lama transformed adversity into opportunity. Rather than turn to bitterness, he made compassion his universal message. He rebuilt Tibetan monastic life in exile, preserved its philosophical schools, and carried its teachings across the world. His gentle humour and humility disarmed sceptics; his laughter, even in the face of loss, became a form of teaching in itself.

Reincarnation, for him, is not merely a matter of doctrine but of responsibility. He describes death as a change of clothes—a continuation of consciousness through new form—and has often said that he will return again "wherever I am needed most." In his public dialogues with scientists, he has encouraged the study of consciousness as a natural continuum, suggesting that rebirth may one day be understood not as miracle but as law.

For Tibetans, his life is proof that compassion itself reincarnates: each Dalai Lama is the same altruistic intention, taking form again and again for the sake of all beings. For the wider world, he stands as a bridge between ancient wisdom and modern reason—a reminder that awakening is not escape from the world's suffering, but a vow to serve within it.

> "Death is just a change of clothes.
> In the next life we take on another body."
> — *PUBLIC TEACHINGS, DHARAMSALA, 1980s*

MAHATMA GANDHI (1869–1948)

BORN	PORBANDAR, GUJARAT, INDIA
DIED	NEW DELHI, INDIA
PROFESSION	POLITICAL LEADER; LAWYER, REFORMER
KNOWN FOR	NONVIOLENT RESISTANCE (AHIMSĀ); LEADERSHIP OF INDIA'S INDEPENDENCE MOVEMENT; SPIRITUAL PHILOSOPHY GROUNDED IN KARMA AND REBIRTH

MOHANDAS KARAMCHAND GANDHI—LATER CALLED MAHATMA, "Great Soul"—stands among the few political leaders whose authority rested not on power but on spiritual conviction. His belief in *ahiṃsā* (nonviolence) and SATYAGRAHA (truth-force) transformed the moral landscape of the twentieth century. Yet beneath his politics lay a vision of life shaped by the ancient doctrines of *karma* and reincarnation—the conviction that the soul endures through countless births and deaths, refining itself through love, sacrifice, and service.

Born into a devout Hindu family in Gujarat, Gandhi's early education was steeped in the *Bhagavad Gītā*, whose verses on duty and detachment remained the touchstone of his philosophy. Trained as a lawyer in London and tested in the racial crucible of South Africa, he came to see every injustice as a mirror of the soul's ignorance. Nonviolence, for him, was not a tactic but an ontological truth: since all beings are bound together in the endless web of rebirth, to harm another is to harm oneself across lifetimes.

Gandhi often spoke of death without fear, describing life as a continuous schooling of the soul. "I cannot think of permanent enmity between man and man," he wrote, "believing as I do in the theory of rebirth." This belief tempered his politics with humility: victory and defeat were transient, but moral integrity endured. His willingness to forgive his oppressors—to meet bullets and prisons with prayer—arose from his faith that divine justice unfolds not in one life but through many.

Reincarnation also shaped his understanding of progress. Humanity, he believed, evolves not through technological advance but through ethical awakening. Each birth is an opportunity to rise a little higher in truth and compassion. In this light, his struggle for Indian independence was not merely national but spiritual—a call for self-purification as the first act of liberation.

When Gandhi fell to an assassin's bullet in 1948, he died with the name of GOD—Rama—on his lips. To his followers, this was not an end but a transition: the soul of the Mahatma, purified through service, returning once more to guide the world toward peace. His life stands as a testament to the power of faith joined with action, and to the enduring Hindu insight that through countless births, the soul learns the meaning of love.

> "I cannot think of permanent enmity between man and man, believing as I do in the theory of rebirth."
> — *YOUNG INDIA*, 1924

WINSTON CHURCHILL (1874–1965)

Born	Blenheim Palace, Oxfordshire, England
Died	London, England
Profession	British Prime Minister; Statesman
Known For	Leadership during WWII; Nobel Prize in Literature

WINSTON CHURCHILL, ARCHITECT OF BRITAIN'S WARTIME resolve and one of the twentieth century's defining figures, was not a man readily associated with mysticism. Yet beneath the armour of logic, rhetoric, and bulldog determination lay a quiet fascination with the idea of reincarnation. Friends and biographers have recorded that Churchill often spoke of having lived before—specifically as a Roman soldier stationed in Britain—a conviction he voiced half in jest yet with a telling sense of familiarity.

His lifelong preoccupation with destiny bordered on metaphysical. From his youth at Sandhurst to the corridors of power, he carried a persistent intuition that his life was part of a larger pattern already set in motion. "I felt as if I were walking with destiny," he wrote on the eve of becoming Prime Minister, "and that all my past life had been but a preparation for this hour." Such words reveal more than patriotism; they hint at a belief that existence unfolds through successive lives, each preparing the ground for the next act of service.

Churchill's imagination often reached beyond the confines of history. His essays on civilisation and empire display an almost cyclical view of human progress—rise, decay, and renewal—echoing ancient notions of rebirth on a collective scale. Though he never formalised these intuitions into doctrine, his casual allusions to past-life memory suggest that reincarnation offered him a language for endurance: the idea that the individual, like the nation, survives catastrophe by being reborn through it.

Those close to him recalled moments when his humour turned philosophical. "I am convinced that I was once a Roman soldier," he would say, adding that the feeling returned most strongly when he walked among Britain's ancient ruins. Whether superstition, self-mythology, or genuine memory, the remark captures something central to Churchill's character—a sense of continuity that defied despair.

In this light, his belief in reincarnation seems less eccentric than emblematic: the statesman who guided Britain through its darkest hour saw time itself as resilient, capable of renewal after ruin. Like the empires he studied and the nations he sought to preserve, he sensed that the human story, too, refuses to end.

> "I am convinced that I was once a Roman soldier."
> — Attributed by friends and biographers
> (e.g. Sir Martin Gilbert)

World Religions & Traditions

You Again

HINDUISM: The Many Rivers of One Tradition

Origin	India (c. 1500 BCE and earlier)
Core Sources	Upaniṣads; Bhagavad Gītā
Central Teaching	Karma and Saṃsāra as shaping forces across lifetimes
Key Themes	Dharma; devotion (Bhakti); cosmic unity; multiplicity within oneness

Hinduism is less a single religion than a confluence of many rivers—ancient ritual, philosophical reflection, and daily devotion merging over thousands of years into one vast spiritual landscape. Its beginnings lie deep in the *Vedic* world of India, around 1500 BCE, when hymns to cosmic order and natural deities were composed in Sanskrit and memorised by generations of priests. These *Vedas* formed the oldest layer of Hindu scripture, concerned more with the maintenance of harmony (*ṛta*) than with individual salvation.

As centuries passed, reflection turned inward. The *Upaniṣads*, mystical dialogues appended to the *Vedas*, began asking not how to appease the gods, but how to understand the self. "What is it," one sage asks, "that when known, everything else is known?" The answer is startlingly simple: the *Ātman*—the innermost Self—is identical with *Brahman*, the infinite reality that pervades all things. To recognise this unity is to awaken from illusion (*māyā*) and to realise that birth and death are but ripples upon an eternal sea.

The Soul and the Wheel of Return

From this revelation grew one of humanity's most intricate visions of continuity. All beings, it teaches, are bound to an immense cycle of birth, death, and rebirth known as *saṃsāra*. Actions in one life sow the seeds of future experience through the moral law of *karma*—a Sanskrit word meaning simply "action." Every thought, word, and deed leaves an imprint, shaping the conditions of the next birth.

Rebirth is not random reward or punishment; it is education. The soul (*jīva*) moves through many bodies as a student moves through grades, refining its understanding until it remembers its own divine nature. Liberation (*mokṣa*) comes when the soul, weary of the round, realises it was never truly separate from the Whole. "As a person casts off worn-out garments and puts on others that are new," says the *Bhagavad Gītā*, "so the embodied soul casts off worn-out bodies and enters others that are new." (2.22)

This image captures the Hindu view of life as both continuous and compassionate: death is change of clothing, not extinction.

Paths Toward Liberation

Because souls differ in temperament and circumstance, Hinduism offers multiple routes to the same summit.

JÑĀNA YOGA, the *way of knowledge*, asks for direct insight into the identity of Ātman and Brahman through disciplined inquiry and meditation.

BHAKTI YOGA, the *way of devotion*, approaches the Divine through love and surrender, seeing GOD as a beloved presence—*Krishna, Śiva,* the Goddess, or the formless Absolute.

KARMA YOGA, the *way of selfless action*, teaches work without attachment to results, transforming duty into worship.

RĀJA YOGA, the *royal path of meditation*, refines body and mind until awareness rests in stillness.

Each path can stand alone or combine with the others. What unites them is the conviction that liberation is not escape from the world but awakening within it—the recognition that spirit pervades even ordinary life.

Living with the Sense of Return

In daily practice, the metaphysics of rebirth becomes lived rhythm. Morning prayers welcome the sun; offerings of food and flowers honour deities whose names vary by region but whose essence is one. The household shrine, more than the temple, is the centre of religion. Festivals mark the cosmic seasons—*Diwali* for light's triumph over darkness, *Holi* for renewal and forgiveness—and each birth, marriage, and death is framed by ritual that ties the individual to the eternal.

Death itself is treated with reverent practicality. The body, regarded as a sacred vessel now returned to nature, is traditionally cremated beside a river. Ashes are scattered in flowing water, a reminder that the soul, too, continues its journey in the current of existence. The mourning period allows the living to perform rites that ease the departed's passage to the next world and, eventually, to rebirth. Through such customs, metaphysical doctrine becomes familial tenderness: continuity is not abstraction but care.

Voices of Scripture

Hindu scriptures speak in many tones—poetic, philosophical, devotional—yet they converge on the same truth of the soul's endurance. The *Kaṭha Upaniṣad* declares:

> "The Self is not born, nor does it die.
> It did not spring from something,
> and nothing sprang from It.
> Unborn, eternal, everlasting, ancient—
> It is not slain when the body is slain."
>
> — *Bhagavad Gītā* (2.18)

And in the *Bhagavad Gītā*, Krishna consoles the warrior Arjuna on the battlefield:

> "Never was there a time when I did not exist,
> nor you, nor these kings;
> nor will there come a time
> when any of us shall cease to be."
>
> — *Bhagavad Gītā* (2.12)

These verses frame reincarnation not as punishment but as assurance: the essence of life cannot be destroyed.

The Modern View and Global Influence

In the nineteenth and twentieth centuries, Hindu teachers carried this vision beyond India. Swami Vivekananda presented it at the World Parliament of Religions in 1893 as a universal philosophy of spiritual evolution. Later, figures such as Paramahansa Yogananda, Sri Aurobindo, and Mahatma Gandhi translated the ancient insight into modern idioms—scientific, political, and ethical. Reincarnation became for many Western readers less a creed than a hypothesis about moral continuity and the growth of consciousness.

Today, within India's diversity, belief in rebirth remains woven into daily life: it underlies compassion toward animals, acceptance of fate, and faith in progress across lives. Whether expressed through philosophy, worship, or quiet moral conduct, the idea persists that every being is on a journey toward remembering its own divine source.

Reflection

Hinduism's great gift to the world is the intuition of unity—that all existence is bound in a single web of being, unfolding through time. Reincarnation is the moral architecture of that unity, ensuring that nothing is lost and everything learned. Seen through this lens, life becomes a vast experiment in awakening: countless births and deaths, all moving toward the realisation that there was never separation to begin with.

To live with such a view is to see the sacred in every creature and every moment—to recognise, as the *Upaniṣads* say, *tat tvam asi*—*"That art Thou."*

Between the Rivers: From Hinduism to Buddhism

From the fertile soil of Hindu thought, another path began to grow—one that shared its reverence for the unseen order of things but questioned its metaphysical foundations. By the time of the Buddha, India was alive with seekers, philosophers, and ascetics testing the limits of human understanding. The great truths of *karma* and rebirth were already well established, yet they had become entangled in speculation about the soul's destiny, the power of ritual, and the hierarchy of caste.

Into this restless landscape stepped Siddhartha Gautama, the future Buddha. He accepted the reality of suffering and rebirth but asked a deeper question: if everything is in motion, what exactly is reborn? His answer was revolutionary. Where the Hindu sage sought to realise the eternal Self, the Buddha pointed instead to the absence of any enduring self—a liberation found not in discovering what we are, but in seeing through what we are not.

With that insight, the wheel of *Dharma* began to turn anew. A tradition was born that would spread from India across Asia and, in time, around the world—carrying with it the quiet, radical message that freedom lies not in eternity, but in awakening.

BUDDHISM: The Turning of the Wheel

ORIGIN	INDIA (5TH CENTURY BCE)
CORE SOURCES	PALI CANON; *DHAMMAPADA*; *NIKĀYAS*
CENTRAL TEACHING	REBIRTH WITHOUT AN ETERNAL SOUL; LIBERATION THROUGH INSIGHT
KEY THEMES	FOUR NOBLE TRUTHS; THE EIGHTFOLD PATH; DEPENDENT ORIGINATION

More than two thousand years ago, on the dusty roads of northern India, a prince named Siddhartha Gautama left his palace in search of an answer to suffering. His quest was not for heaven, nor for metaphysical truth, but for understanding the human condition. After years of austerity and meditation beneath the *Bodhi* tree, he awoke to insight: life is impermanent, craving binds us to its wheel, and freedom lies in seeing things as they truly are. From that awakening he became known as the Buddha—"the Awakened One"—and his teaching, the *Dharma*, began a turning of the wheel that would reshape spiritual history.

What the Buddha discovered was neither faith in divine intervention nor denial of life's meaning, but a middle way between extremes. He saw that existence unfolds through cause and effect; that every thought, word, and deed conditions what follows; and that this continuity extends beyond a single lifetime. The doctrine of rebirth in Buddhism is not about a permanent soul migrating from body to body, but about the flow of consciousness—a river of moments, each giving rise to the next. When ignorance and craving persist, the current continues. When they cease, the river finds its stillness in *nibbāna* (*nirvāṇa*).

What is Reborn?

This question puzzled early disciples as much as later scholars. If there is no immortal soul (*attā*), what carries on after death? The Buddha replied with the image of one flame lighting another: there is continuity without identity. The person who is reborn is neither exactly the same nor entirely different—a process, not an entity.

Buddhism analyses this process into five aggregates (*skandhas*): form, feeling, perception, mental formations, and consciousness. Together they create the illusion of a solid self. When the body dies, the momentum of these mental energies—shaped by *karma*—generates new conditions for consciousness to arise. In this way, rebirth is a natural extension of causality, not an act of divine will. It is the law of nature applied to mind.

> "No maker of the world am I,
> Nor one who runs within it;
> For me there is no coming or going—
> Thus the end of birth is known."
>
> — *Sutta Nipāta* 5.6

The Wheel of Life

To illustrate this continual motion, Buddhist tradition depicts the *bhavachakra*—the Wheel of Life. Around its rim turn the six realms of rebirth: gods, demigods, humans, animals, hungry ghosts, and hell-beings. Each realm mirrors a psychological state—pride, jealousy, contentment, ignorance, craving, or hatred—and each being moves through them as consciousness evolves. At the wheel's hub spin three animals: a pig, a cock, and a snake—ignorance, greed, and aversion—the forces that keep the cycle turning.

In this cosmology, human birth is considered the rarest and most precious. It balances pleasure and pain in just the right measure to motivate practice. The chance of attaining such a life, says the Buddha, is like a blind turtle surfacing once every hundred years and finding its head through a floating yoke on the ocean. To waste it is to waste eons of opportunity.

The Law of Karma

Karma, in Buddhism, means intentional action. Every deliberate thought or deed plants a seed that will bear fruit in future experience. This law is not moral in the sense of reward and punishment; it is descriptive, like gravity. If anger is sown, suffering follows; if compassion is cultivated, peace arises.

The key lies in intention. Actions done with greed, hatred, or delusion strengthen the chain of rebirth. Those done with generosity, kindness, and clarity loosen it. Freedom comes not by divine grace but by understanding cause and effect so thoroughly that craving loses its grip. The Buddha summed this up in one verse:

> "Mind precedes all things; mind is their chief; they are made by mind. If one speaks or acts with a pure mind, happiness follows like a shadow that never departs."
>
> — *Dhammapada* 1–2

Paths to Liberation

The Buddha's teaching is often compared to a physician's prescription: diagnose suffering, understand its cause, see that it can cease, and follow the cure. These four insights—the Four Noble Truths—form the foundation of all Buddhist schools. The path leading out of suffering is the Noble Eightfold Path: right view, intention, speech, action, livelihood, effort, mindfulness, and concentration.

Through meditation, ethical conduct, and insight, the practitioner weakens the forces that perpetuate rebirth. When ignorance is extinguished, the wheel stops turning. The flame goes out—not into darkness, but into peace beyond duality. This is *nibbāna*: unconditioned freedom, the end of becoming.

Mahāyāna and Vajrayāna Visions

As Buddhism spread across Asia, new interpretations blossomed. In the *Mahāyāna* traditions of China, Korea, and Japan, the highest ideal became the *Bodhisattva*—the one who, though capable of enlightenment, vows to return again and again until all beings are free. Here, rebirth is not bondage but compassion in motion. Each life is another chance to serve.

In Tibet, Buddhism evolved into the *Vajrayāna*, or "Diamond Way," rich in symbolism and visionary maps of the afterlife. Texts such as the *Bardo Thödol* (popularly known as The Tibetan Book of the Dead) describe states of consciousness between death and rebirth—the *bardos*—where the mind encounters its own luminous and terrifying projections. Liberation, these teachings say, remains possible even after death, if one recognises these visions as one's own nature.

Living and Dying with Awareness

For Buddhists, meditation on death is not morbid but clarifying. To remember impermanence is to live more fully. Monks contemplate the decay of the body; lay followers reflect daily on the certainty of death and the uncertainty of its time. This practice dissolves denial and strengthens compassion.

When death comes, families gather to chant, recall good deeds, and dedicate merit—the positive energy of virtuous acts—to the one who has passed. In

Tibet and parts of Southeast Asia, texts are read aloud to guide the departing consciousness. The mood is not despair but mindful accompaniment: the traveller moves on, the living continue the work of understanding.

A Universal Teaching

Beyond its rituals and cosmologies, Buddhism offers a profoundly psychological insight: that rebirth is happening moment by moment. Each instant of craving gives rise to the next, creating the illusion of a continuous "self." To observe this directly—in meditation, in daily reaction, in the play of thought—is to see the mechanism of rebirth in miniature. Freedom does not depend on future lives; it begins now, in each moment we cease to cling.

This insight transcends culture. Whether one believes in literal rebirth or sees it as metaphor, the message is the same: actions have consequences, compassion matters, and awareness can transform suffering.

Reflection

Buddhism's genius lies in turning the grand question of afterlife into a laboratory of the present. Instead of asking where we go after death, it asks why we are not yet free while alive. Reincarnation here is less a promise of eternity than a challenge to wake up within the cycle itself.

To live as the Buddha taught is to recognise impermanence in every breath, to meet each moment with compassion, and to realise that the line between this life and the next may be thinner than the pause between thoughts. In that recognition, the wheel of birth and death begins to slow—and, perhaps, to stop.

You Again

JAINISM: THE RELIGION OF NON-VIOLENCE

ORIGIN	INDIA (6TH CENTURY BCE)
CORE SOURCES	ĀGAMAS; TATTVĀRTHA SŪTRA
CENTRAL TEACHING	THE SOUL PROGRESSES THROUGH COUNTLESS REBIRTHS TOWARD LIBERATION
KEY THEMES	RADICAL NON-VIOLENCE; TRUTH; AUSTERITY; KARMA AS A MATERIAL SUBSTANCE

ALONGSIDE HINDUISM AND BUDDHISM, JAINISM IS ONE OF INDIA'S three ancient spiritual traditions. Its roots reach back to the same age of wandering ascetics and philosophical ferment that gave rise to the Buddha. The Jains trace their lineage through a line of twenty-four *Tīrthaṅkaras*—"ford-makers," those who have crossed the stream of suffering and shown others the way. The most recent of these, Mahāvīra (6th century BCE), was a contemporary of the Buddha and taught an uncompromising vision of non-violence, truth, and self-restraint.

For the Jains, life in all its forms—from the smallest microbe to the loftiest god—possesses a soul (*jīva*). Each soul is inherently pure, luminous, and endowed with infinite knowledge and bliss. Yet, bound by matter and ignorance, it becomes entangled in the cycle of birth and death (*saṃsāra*). Liberation (*mokṣa*) is achieved when every trace of karmic matter is shed and the soul rises, weightless, to the summit of the cosmos, where it abides forever in omniscient stillness.

Karma as Substance

In Jain philosophy, *karma* is not merely moral causation but a kind of subtle physical dust that clings to the soul whenever one acts with passion, violence, or deceit. Even the smallest act of harm binds the soul to the wheel of rebirth. Hence the central ethic of Jainism: *ahiṃsā*—non-injury to all living beings. Monks and nuns practise this principle with exquisite care, sweeping the path before them to avoid treading on insects, wearing cloth masks to prevent inhaling tiny organisms, and restricting possessions to the bare minimum.

Lay followers, too, are guided by vows of non-violence, truthfulness, honesty, chastity, and non-attachment. Vegetarianism is near-universal, and compassion extends to the smallest creatures. In this radical empathy, Jainism represents one of humanity's earliest ecological visions—seeing the universe as a vast web of interdependent life, where harm to one being reverberates through all.

The Journey of the Soul

Rebirth in Jain cosmology follows precise laws. Depending on one's karmic weight, the soul may be reborn in heavenly, human, animal, or hellish realms. The process is endless until self-discipline burns away every impurity. When the final bonds are cut, the liberated soul (*siddha*) ascends to the top of the universe—a realm beyond time, neither heaven nor place, known as *Siddhaśilā*. There, infinite awareness shines unobstructed.

> "The soul comes alone and goes alone,
> It has no companion;
> Whatever it does, good or evil,
> It must bear the fruit of its own deeds."
>
> — *Uttarādhyayana Sūtra* 23.56

Reflection

Jainism offers a vision of existence both austere and luminous. Where Hinduism celebrates unity and Buddhism emphasises awareness, Jainism insists on responsibility. Every act—however small—leaves its trace upon the soul. Liberation, therefore, is not granted by grace but earned through purity of thought, word, and deed. To live as a Jain is to see life everywhere and to tread the earth as lightly as possible, knowing that every breath can either bind or free.

> "The soul is eternal. It is born again and again, experiencing the fruits of its own actions."
> — *Tattvārtha Sūtra* 2.10

You Again

OF THE WISE & GLORIOUS

SIKHISM: A FAITH OF ONENESS

ORIGIN	PUNJAB (LATE 15TH CENTURY CE)
CORE SOURCES	*GURU GRANTH SAHIB; DASAM GRANTH*
CENTRAL TEACHING	UNION WITH THE ONE THROUGH REMEMBRANCE AND ETHICAL LIVING
KEY THEMES	EQUALITY; SERVICE (*SEVA*); COMMUNITY; DIVINE PRESENCE IN ALL

SIKHISM AROSE IN FIFTEENTH-CENTURY PUNJAB—A FERTILE MEETING ground of Hindu, Muslim, and Sufi ideas—during a period of deep social division. Caste hierarchy, ritual excess, and religious rivalry left many seekers disillusioned. Into this world was born Guru Nanak (1469–1539), a poet and mystic whose insight was at once simple and revolutionary. After years of contemplation, he emerged from a visionary experience declaring:

"There is no Hindu, there is no Muslim."

— GURU NANAK

This single sentence became the seed of a new spiritual movement founded on the unity of GOD and the equality of all human beings. Sikhism, from the Sanskrit *śiṣya* meaning "disciple," calls its followers *Sikhs*—learners on the path of truth. Its scripture, the Guru Granth Sahib, collects over five thousand hymns by Guru Nanak and the nine Gurus who succeeded him, along with verses from Hindu and Muslim saints whose words resonated with the same spirit of devotion.

At its heart lies the affirmation of a single, formless Creator— *Ik Oṅkār* ("One Reality")—expressed in the opening line of the *Japji Sahib*:

112

> "There is One Reality, the Eternal Truth,
> Creator, without fear, without enmity,
> Timeless, unborn, self-existent,
> realised by the Guru's grace."
>
> — *Japji Sahib*

The Divine and the Soul

In Sikh philosophy, the universe is an emanation of this One Reality. All forms of life are waves upon the same ocean, animated by the Divine Light (*jot*). The soul (*ātma*) is not separate from GOD but forgets its origin through attachment and ego (*haumai*). This forgetfulness is the root of bondage and the reason for rebirth. Each life is an opportunity for remembrance—to awaken to the truth that the Beloved is within all.

Sikhism accepts the ancient Indian idea of reincarnation but recasts it in the language of devotion and grace. The soul wanders through many births and deaths (*janam maran*)—said poetically to number 8.4 million forms—until divine remembrance dawns. Liberation (*mukti*) is not achieved by ritual purity or ascetic withdrawal but by dissolving the ego in the love of GOD. When the illusion of separateness ends, the soul merges with the Divine like a drop returning to the ocean.

> "As water merges with water,
> Light merges with light,
> The soul unites with the Lord,
> And is freed from birth and death."
>
> — *Guru Granth Sahib*, 278

Karma and Grace

Sikhism, like Hinduism and Jainism, teaches that one's actions (*karma*) shape the conditions of life. Yet *karma* alone cannot grant freedom. Only through GOD's grace (*nadar*) does the gate of liberation open. The balance between moral law and divine mercy gives Sikhism its unique warmth: deeds matter, but not as accounting—they prepare the heart for grace.

Guru Nanak expressed this balance beautifully:

> "By the *karma* of past actions
> the robe of this body is obtained,
> By His grace the gate of liberation is found."
> — *Guru Granth Sahib*, 2

Thus, life is both responsibility and gift—a chance to align human effort with divine compassion.

The Way of the Gurmukh

The purpose of Sikh life is to become *gurmukh*—one whose face is turned toward the Guru, or Truth. Its opposite is *manmukh*—one who follows the restless dictates of ego. The *gurmukh* lives in awareness of GOD through three central disciplines:

Nām Simran—constant remembrance of the Divine Name. This is the essence of Sikh meditation: repeating and dwelling in the vibration of GOD's presence, often through the sacred syllable *Wāheguru* ("Wondrous Lord").

Kīrat Karnī—honest labour and integrity in daily work. Spiritual life is not separate from worldly responsibility; one earns one's living righteously and shares the fruit.

VAND CHAKNA—generosity and community service, symbolised by the communal kitchen (*langar*), where all sit and eat together as equals.

These three pillars bind devotion to daily life. The goal is not renunciation but participation with awareness—to live fully in the world without being consumed by it.

The Ten Gurus and the Living Word

After Guru Nanak, nine successive Gurus guided the Sikh community, refining its organisation and ethics. The tenth, Guru Gobind Singh (1666-1708), transformed the Sikhs into a disciplined fellowship—the *Khalsa*—dedicated to courage, equality, and the defence of the oppressed. He instructed that after his passing there would be no human successor: the eternal Guru would henceforth be the Guru Granth Sahib, the scripture itself.

This text is treated not merely as a book but as the living voice of GOD. It is enthroned in every *gurdwara* (temple), where it is recited, sung, and revered. Its language is musical and inclusive: alongside the Sikh Gurus' own hymns are verses by Hindu *bhaktas* and Muslim Sufis such as Kabir and Sheikh Farid, expressing the same truth that GOD transcends religion.

Ethics and the Equality of All

Sikhism is radically egalitarian. It rejects caste, ritual purity, and gender hierarchy. Men and women stand equal before the Divine; both may lead worship, sing hymns, and share in all roles. The turban, uncut hair, and the five symbols (*kakkars*) worn by the initiated serve not to set Sikhs apart but to remind them of discipline, dignity, and readiness to serve others.

The *langar*, or free communal meal, remains one of the faith's most visible expressions of equality. Instituted by Guru Nanak, it ensures that no one who enters a *gurdwara* leaves hungry. The act of eating together symbolises the dissolution of barriers—spiritual practice made tangible.

Life, Death, and Liberation

In Sikh thought, death is a return, not an ending. The body is a garment, worn for a while and laid aside. The soul continues its journey according to its awareness and deeds. At the moment of death, remembrance of the Divine Name is paramount; it guides the soul through transition. The Sikh funeral (*Antim Ardās*) is therefore a service of gratitude, not lament—a collective prayer that the soul rest in union with GOD.

The Guru Granth Sahib reminds believers that liberation need not wait for death. To live in remembrance of the Divine, to act without ego, and to see GOD in all beings is to taste *mukti* here and now. The cycle of birth and death continues only for those who forget.

> "Those who remember the Lord in their hearts
> Are liberated from birth and death;
> They merge in the Eternal,
> And their coming and going cease."
> — GURU GRANTH SAHIB, 11

A Living Faith

Today, Sikhism counts over thirty million adherents worldwide, forming vibrant communities across India, the United Kingdom, North America, and beyond. Wherever Sikhs settle, they build gurdwaras not only as places of worship but as centres of education, service, and hospitality. From feeding the hungry during natural disasters to supporting local charities, *Sevā* (selfless service) remains the heartbeat of the faith.

For Sikhs, reincarnation is not a theory of cosmic mechanics but a mirror held to the soul. Each birth is an invitation to grow in humility and compassion; each death, a reminder of the nearness of GOD. The purpose of life is not to escape the world but to sanctify it through remembrance, service, and love.

Reflection

Sikhism stands as a bridge between the mysticism of the East and the monotheism of the West. It embraces the ancient Indian understanding of *karma* and rebirth, yet places them within a theology of grace. Where Hinduism speaks of self-realisation and Buddhism of awakening, Sikhism speaks of remembrance—of knowing, through love, the One who was never absent.

To live as a Sikh is to walk through the world awake to its sacredness: to work honestly, share generously, and keep the Name alive upon the tongue and in the heart. When remembrance is perfect, the cycle ends, and the soul returns home—not to some distant heaven, but to the infinite Presence it never truly left.

KABBALAH: COVENANT & MYSTERY OF LIFE

ORIGIN	MEDIEVAL SPAIN (13TH CENTURY CE)
CORE SOURCES	SHA'AR HA-GILGULIM; ZOHAR
CENTRAL TEACHING	GILGUL NESHAMOT — TRANSMIGRATION OF SOULS
KEY THEMES	REPAIR OF THE WORLD (TIKKUN OLAM); ASCENT OF THE SOUL; DIVINE EMANATIONS

JUDAISM, THE OLDEST OF THE WORLD'S MONOTHEISTIC RELIGIONS, begins not with a philosophy of the soul but with a story—a people called into relationship with the ONE GOD. The Hebrew Bible does not speculate at length about life after death; its focus is covenant, justice, and remembrance. GOD is not a distant abstraction but a living presence who speaks, commands, and accompanies humanity through history.

Abraham's call, Moses's liberation of the Israelites, and the giving of the Law at Sinai all express one idea: that holiness is found not in escape from the world but in faithful participation within it. The Jewish path is one of *mitzvot*—commandments that sanctify ordinary life. Eating, resting, working, and speaking all become opportunities to reflect divine order.

In the early scriptures, immortality is collective rather than personal. A person lives on through family, tribe, and memory. The dead "sleep with their ancestors" in the shadowy realm of *Sheol*, awaiting GOD'S renewal. Yet the seeds of a deeper vision were already there: if GOD is just, and life often unjust, there must be a continuation in which divine justice is fulfilled. That intuition would flower centuries later in prophetic and mystical thought.

The Soul in Scripture and Tradition

The Hebrew word for soul, *nefesh*, originally meant "breath" or "life-force." To be alive was to breathe the breath that God breathed into Adam: "Then the Lord God formed man from the dust of the ground, and breathed into his nostrils the breath of life, and the man became a living soul." (Genesis 2:7)

Over time, Jewish reflection identified multiple dimensions of that soul—*nefesh* (vital force), *ruach* (spirit or emotion), and *neshamah* (divine essence). These layers describe not separate entities but the gradations of consciousness through which human beings relate to God.

In the Second Temple period (roughly 500 BCE–70 CE), new ideas entered Jewish thought through contact with Persian and Hellenistic philosophies. Concepts of resurrection, judgment, and reward began to take shape. The Book of Daniel (12:2) speaks for the first time of a future awakening: "Many of those who sleep in the dust of the earth shall awake, some to everlasting life, and some to shame and everlasting contempt."

From this point on, Jewish tradition diverged in two directions—one affirming resurrection at the end of time, the other exploring reincarnation as a continuous process of the soul's return.

The Kabbalistic Vision

Reincarnation (*gilgul neshamot,* "rolling of souls") enters Judaism most clearly through the Kabbalah, the mystical stream that blossomed in medieval Spain and the Holy Land. For the Kabbalists, the universe is a dynamic outflow of divine energy (*Ein Sof*—"the Infinite"), refracted through ten attributes or *sefirot*. Human beings, created in the image of these attributes, participate in restoring balance when they act justly—a process known as *tikkun olam*, "repairing the world."

Within this cosmic vision, the soul's journey extends beyond one lifetime. A soul may return again and again to complete its unfinished work, to repair wrongs, or to elevate sparks of holiness trapped in the material world. The 16th-century mystic Isaac Luria of Safed systematised this doctrine, teaching that every soul has a specific purpose, and reincarnation is the mercy that allows it to fulfil that purpose.

> "Know that souls are subject to transmigration,
> and people do not know the ways of the HOLY ONE, blessed be He.
> They do not know that they come to be rectified time after time."
>
> — ISAAC LURIA, *SHA'AR HAGILGULIM*

In this light, reincarnation is not punishment but opportunity. The soul returns not to suffer but to heal—to re-align itself and the world with divine wholeness.

LIFE, DEATH, AND THE WORLD TO COME

Mainstream Judaism holds a spectrum of views about what happens after death. Some emphasise resurrection—the renewal of the body in a redeemed world; others speak of the World to Come (*Olam Ha-Ba*) as a purely spiritual state of communion with GOD. The *Talmud* captures this diversity with characteristic humility: "All Israel has a share in the World to Come, but the righteous of all nations too have a share."

The afterlife is never central to Jewish faith. What matters is how one lives here and now—fulfilling commandments, practising mercy, pursuing justice, studying Torah, and blessing life. Yet even within this practical orientation, the sense of continuity endures. In many Jewish prayers for the dead, the soul is described as "bound up in the bond of life" (*tzrur b'tzror ha-chayim*)—a poetic assurance that consciousness is not extinguished but gathered back into the living GOD.

Death and Remembrance

Jewish mourning customs reflect both realism and hope. The body is treated with utmost respect: washed, wrapped in a plain linen shroud, and buried swiftly, affirming that death is part of the natural order. Mourners recite the Kaddish, not to petition for the dead, but to magnify and sanctify GOD'S name—an act of praise amid loss. The rhythm of grief is given shape by defined periods: *shivah* (seven days), *shloshim* (thirty days), and the annual *yahrzeit*, when a candle is lit in memory. Through remembrance, the living sustain the bond between worlds.

Mystical writings expand this ritual tenderness into metaphysical poetry. The soul, say the Kabbalists, lingers near the body for several days before ascending. It then journeys through subtle realms of purification until it finds its place of rest—or returns, if unfinished, to another life. The prayers of the living, acts of charity, and study of sacred texts are said to assist this passage.

Reflection

Judaism's power lies in its balance between the immediate and the eternal. It begins with ethics and ends with mystery. The Hebrew prophets taught that justice and compassion are the true sacrifices God desires; the mystics added that every act of love repairs a fragment of creation. Whether understood as resurrection, reunion, or reincarnation, the afterlife in Judaism is not a distant heaven but the continuation of covenant—the unbroken dialogue between God and the soul.

Where Hinduism speaks of the self's identity with the Absolute, and Buddhism of the cessation of craving, Judaism speaks of relationship. The soul's journey is not toward dissolution but communion; not the extinction of individuality, but its fulfilment in divine love.

In the words of the *Zohar*, the great book of Jewish mysticism:

> "The soul of man is the lamp of the Lord;
> Through it, He searches the chambers of the heart.
> When the light burns clear,
> It rejoices to return to its source."

You Again

CHRISTIANITY: THE PROMISE OF RESURRECTION

ORIGIN	1ST CENTURY CE, ROMAN JUDEA
CORE SOURCES	NEW TESTAMENT
CENTRAL TEACHING	RESURRECTION THROUGH DIVINE GRACE; CHRISTIANITY TEACHES RESURRECTION, NOT REINCARNATION
KEY THEMES	REDEMPTION, TRANSFORMATION, MORAL RENEWAL

CHRISTIANITY BEGINS NOT WITH A DOCTRINE BUT WITH AN EVENT— the life, death, and resurrection of Jesus of Nazareth. To his followers, that resurrection was not metaphor but revelation: the assurance that death is not the end, and that divine love is stronger than mortality. The earliest Christian proclamation, echoing through the letters of Saint Paul, was simple and audacious: "Christ is risen from the dead, the first fruits of those who have fallen asleep." (1 CORINTHIANS 15:20)

This conviction shaped everything that followed. In Jewish thought, the righteous awaited a bodily resurrection "at the end of days." Christianity reinterpreted that hope in personal terms: the resurrection had already begun in Jesus, and those united with him would share in it. Life was not a cycle of returns but a journey toward renewal—one life, one death, one rising into communion with GOD.

THE SOUL AND ETERNAL LIFE

The New Testament speaks of the *psychē* (soul) and *pneuma* (spirit) not as detachable parts but as aspects of a single living person animated by GOD'S breath. Salvation is therefore holistic: body and soul redeemed together. "The Word became flesh," wrote the evangelist John, "and dwelt among us"—a declaration that matter itself can bear the divine.

Early Christian communities, spread across the Mediterranean, debated how the immortal soul and the mortal body were related. Influenced by Greek philosophy, some theologians, such as Origen of Alexandria (3rd century CE), speculated that the soul pre-existed the body and might return to new embodiments as it matured toward perfection. His vast *On First Principles* spoke of the soul's long education through the ages—a view resembling reincarnation in spirit if not in detail. Later Church councils, however, condemned this teaching, fearing it undermined the uniqueness of Christ's incarnation and the moral urgency of a single earthly life.

Mainstream doctrine therefore affirmed resurrection, not reincarnation: the same person restored by God's power, transformed but continuous with the one who lived and died.

The Diversity of the Early Church

The first centuries of Christianity were a time of remarkable diversity. Alongside emerging orthodoxy flourished a family of movements later called Gnostic—seekers of gnosis, inner knowledge of divine reality. Gnostic texts, many rediscovered at *Nag Hammadi* in 1945, portrayed the material world as a realm of ignorance from which the soul must awaken.

In several of these writings, the soul's journey involves repeated embodiments. The *Pistis Sophia*, for instance, describes souls ascending through the heavens according to their purity, while those still bound by desire "wander through the world in different bodies." The recently unearthed GOSPEL OF JUDAS (2nd century CE) presents Judas not as traitor but as the disciple who understands that spirit is trapped in flesh and must be released. It hints at a cosmic cycle of generation and release—the soul passing through forms until it returns to its luminous origin.

These texts reveal that early Christian thought was not monolithic. Some communities saw salvation as a gradual unveiling across lifetimes; others as a decisive transformation in one. The eventual victory of orthodoxy narrowed the spectrum but did not erase the memory of these alternative visions.

Medieval and Mystical Currents

Although the official Church rejected reincarnation, mystical and esoteric currents kept the question alive. In the 12th century, certain Christian Kabbalists and later the Brethren of the Free Spirit in Europe spoke of the soul's progressive purification through successive lives. Renaissance thinkers such as Giovanni Pico della Mirandola and Giordano Bruno drew on Platonic and Hermetic sources to propose a universe of infinite worlds and evolving souls—ideas that anticipated modern notions of spiritual evolution.

In the Eastern Orthodox tradition, a subtler continuity survived: the soul's passage through aerial toll-houses or stages of purification after death. Though not reincarnation, it reflects the same awareness that the soul's growth transcends a single moment. Christian mystics from Meister Eckhart to Jacob Böhme spoke of the "birth of God in the soul," an interior resurrection that occurs again and again within a single life—transformation as cyclical renewal rather than literal return.

Life, Death, and the Hope of Glory

At the heart of Christian faith remains the conviction that creation itself will be redeemed. Death is an enemy already conquered in Christ; the cosmos will one day share in that victory. The *Nicene Creed* still affirms, "I look for the resurrection of the dead and the life of the world to come." For believers, this is not metaphor but promise: the same love that raised Jesus will raise all who live in that love.

Funeral liturgies therefore speak the language of hope: "In sure and certain hope of the resurrection to eternal life." The dead are commended to God's mercy, the living reminded that eternal life begins even now, whenever love triumphs over fear. Saints and mystics describe heaven not as distant place but as union—*theosis*—participation in the divine life.

Reflection

Christianity's gift to the wider conversation about rebirth is its vision of transformation through relationship. Where Hinduism sees an eternal self seeking union with the Absolute, and Buddhism a stream of causes seeking cessation, Christianity sees a beloved creature called into communion with its Creator. Time itself becomes redemptive—history moving toward fulfilment, not repetition.

Yet at its edges, in the whispers of the Gnostics and the insights of mystics, the idea of many lives persisted as a symbol of GOD'S endless patience. Whether one life or many, the message is the same: the soul is being shaped for love. In the words of St Paul,

> "We all, with unveiled faces,
> beholding as in a mirror the glory of the LORD,
> are being transformed into the same image from glory to glory."
>
> — 2 CORINTHIANS 3:18

To live in that spirit is already to taste resurrection—a daily dying to ignorance, a daily rising into light.

ISLAM (SUFI POETIC): THE DAY OF RETURN

ORIGIN	7TH CENTURY CE, ARABIA
CORE SOURCES	QUR'AN; SUFI MYSTICAL POETRY AND COMMENTARIES
CENTRAL TEACHING	RESURRECTION BEFORE GOD; JOURNEY OF THE SOUL TOWARD UNION— ISLAM TEACHES RESURRECTION, NOT REINCARNATION
KEY THEMES	DIVINE REMEMBRANCE; PURIFICATION; SURRENDER (*ISLĀM*)

ISLAM BEGINS WITH A DECLARATION OF UNITY—LĀ ILĀHA ILLĀ ALLĀH: "There is no god but GOD."

Everything else flows from that single truth. Creation, revelation, and judgment are all expressions of the same divine reality. Human life is a trust (*amānah*) bestowed by GOD, and death is not an annihilation but a return: "Indeed we belong to GOD, and to Him we shall return." (*Qurʾān* 2:156)

From the earliest revelations to the Prophet Muḥammad (570–632 CE), Islam has affirmed that every soul is created once, lives one earthly life, dies, and will be resurrected for judgment. The *Qurʾān* speaks repeatedly of this "Day of Resurrection" (*Yawm al-Qiyāmah*) when all beings will be gathered and their deeds weighed in the balance. The righteous enter paradise (*Jannah*), described as gardens beneath which rivers flow; the unjust face purification or loss.

Unlike the cyclic cosmologies of India, Islam envisions a linear journey— from creation to accountability to eternal life. The emphasis is moral rather than metaphysical: what matters is not remembering past lives but living this one with sincerity, justice, and mercy.

The Nature of the Soul

The *Qur'ān* portrays the soul (*nafs*) as a subtle essence breathed into humanity by GOD Himself:

> "When I have fashioned him
> and breathed into him of My spirit,
> fall down before him in prostration."
>
> — *QUR'ĀN* 15:29

The soul is therefore both created and divine in origin—not a fragment of GOD, but animated by His breath. It is tested through life's circumstances, pulled between lower impulses (*nafs al-ammārah*, the commanding self) and higher awareness (*nafs al-muṭma'innah*, the tranquil soul). Salvation means purification of the self, the alignment of will with the divine will (*islām* literally means "surrender").

When death arrives, the soul enters *barzakh*—an intermediate realm between death and resurrection. There, it experiences a foretaste of its ultimate destiny. The *Qur'ān* does not describe *barzakh* as a cycle of rebirth, but later Islamic philosophers and mystics expanded the metaphor into subtler forms of continuation.

Philosophical Interpretations

Classical Muslim thinkers such as Avicenna (Ibn Sīnā) and al-Ghazālī explored the soul's immortality in rational and mystical terms. Avicenna described the soul as immaterial and self-aware—"a substance subsisting by itself." While he rejected literal transmigration, he proposed that souls progress through stages of refinement toward pure intellect. Al-Ghazālī, reconciling philosophy and faith, taught that death is a mirror: each person beholds the reality they have inwardly cultivated.

These reflections show how deeply Islam values intention (*niyyah*). Every act, however small, carries moral consequence because it reveals the state of the heart. The cosmic order is just: no deed is lost, no life meaningless.

THE SUFI VISION—CYCLES OF TRANSFORMATION

Within Sufism, the inner path of Islam, rebirth takes on a spiritual rather than biological meaning. The Sufis speak of dying before death—"*Mutū qabla an tamūtū*"—dying to the ego so that the divine life may awaken within. In this sense, reincarnation becomes an interior process: the soul is born and dies many times within one lifetime as it sheds its veils of forgetfulness.

Jalāl al-Dīn Rūmī (1207–1273), the great Persian poet-mystic, expressed this in language that echoes the Indian understanding of continuous transformation:

> "I died as a mineral and became a plant,
> I died as plant and rose to animal,
> I died as animal and I was man.
> Why should I fear? When was I less by dying?"
> — *MASNAVĪ*, BOOK III

Rūmī's verses are not doctrinal but symbolic, describing the soul's ascent through states of consciousness toward divine union. Other Sufi masters, such as Ibn ʿArabī, taught that existence is a ceaseless self-disclosure of GOD (*tajallī*). Each form in creation is a manifestation of the divine Names, and the soul moves through these forms as it learns to recognise its Beloved. What appears as many births is, in truth, the One Life revealing itself in endless ways.

Death and the Afterlife

In Islamic teaching, death is a passage overseen by angels. At the moment of separation, the angel of death (*Malak al-Mawt*) calls the righteous soul gently:

> "O serene soul, return to your Lord,
> pleased and pleasing."
>
> — *Qur'ān* 89:27–28)

The deceased are washed, wrapped in white cloth, and buried facing Mecca—a gesture of humility and orientation toward the Divine. The community gathers to recite the *Janāzah* prayer, which includes no eulogy, only supplication for mercy and peace.

Paradise is portrayed in vivid imagery—gardens, cool shade, flowing water—but these symbols point beyond the physical. The real paradise, say the mystics, is proximity to GOD; the real hell, separation from Him. The *Ḥadīth* (sayings of the Prophet) describe the hereafter as the unveiling of truth: the veils fall, and every soul beholds what it truly loved.

Reincarnation and the Boundaries of Orthodoxy

Islamic orthodoxy does not accept reincarnation (tanāsukh) in the literal sense of a soul re-entering new bodies. The *Qur'ān* explicitly denies a return to worldly life after death:

> "When death comes to one of them, he says, 'My Lord, send me back.' But no! It is but a word he speaks; behind them is a barrier until the Day they are resurrected."
>
> —*Qur'ān* 23:99-100)

Nevertheless, the metaphor of rebirth persists at the heart of Islamic spirituality. The human journey is seen as one vast cycle of descent and return—from GOD, through creation, back to GOD again. Sufi poets often describe multiple lives as stages of awareness rather than separate incarnations: the soul passes through mineral, plant, animal, and human states as symbols of increasing consciousness.

In this way, Islam preserves linear resurrection while still acknowledging cyclical transformation. Every prayer, every act of repentance, every remembrance (*dhikr*) is a small resurrection—a return to life from the sleep of forgetfulness.

Reflection

Islam unites the moral clarity of monotheism with the mystical depth of inner transformation. It rejects the notion of endless rebirth but embraces the essence of rebirth as renewal of the heart. Death is not feared but understood as reunion; life is a trust to be lived with awareness of accountability.

Where Hinduism envisions liberation through self-realisation, and Buddhism through insight, Islam offers surrender: freedom through submission to the Beloved's will. And within that surrender, Sufism whispers a subtler secret—that every moment of love, every act of remembrance, is itself a return to the Source.

> "He brings the living out of the dead and the dead out of the living;
> He revives the earth after its death—thus shall you be brought forth."
>
> — *Qur'ān* 30:19

You Again

To live by that verse is to see resurrection everywhere: in the turning of seasons, in repentance after error, in the awakening of the heart that remembers it has never been apart from GOD.

DAOISM: THE WAY THAT CANNOT BE SPOKEN

ORIGIN	CHINA (4TH–3RD CENTURY BCE)
CORE SOURCES	*DAO DE JING*; *ZHUANGZI*
CENTRAL TEACHING	LIVING IN ACCORD WITH THE DAO, THE SPONTANEOUS NATURAL ORDER
KEY THEMES	YIN–YANG BALANCE; SIMPLICITY; NON-STRIVING (*WU WEI*)

IN ANCIENT CHINA, LONG BEFORE BUDDHISM CROSSED THE HIMALAYAS or Confucius codified ethics, the sages of the valleys spoke quietly of a Way that moves through all things. They called it the *Dao*—the Way, the pattern, the source. Its essence cannot be grasped or named, for every name already divides what is seamless.

> "The Dao that can be spoken is not the eternal Dao.
> The name that can be named is not the eternal name."
> — *DAO DE JING* 1

Daoism (or Taoism) began as this insight—a poetic philosophy rather than a religion. In the writings of Laozi (Lao Tzu) and Zhuangzi, the Dao is the uncreated origin of heaven and earth, the pulse that gives rise to all forms and receives them back without effort or judgment. Life and death, being and non-being, are seen as alternating expressions of the same rhythm. The wise person does not cling to life or fear death, but moves with the current of transformation.

Transformation, Not Reincarnation

In the early classics, there is no mention of personal reincarnation as found in India. Instead, there is transformation (*hua*). The world is a ceaseless metamorphosis of energy (*qi*), and every creature a temporary knot in its flow. When a person dies, their vital energy disperses, returning to the larger field of the Dao. To resist this process is folly; to accept it is wisdom.

> "Life and death are companions;
> being and non-being arise together.
> Therefore the sage makes no distinctions."
>
> — Zhuangzi 2

The story is told of Zhuangzi, who, when his wife died, sat beating a drum and singing. When asked why he did not mourn, he answered that she had simply changed form: from formlessness to birth, from birth to death, and back again to the great transformation. To grieve excessively was to misunderstand the natural way of things.

Here lies the essence of Daoist teaching on continuity: nothing truly ends, nothing is truly born. The universe breathes itself in and out eternally.

The Souls Within

As Daoism evolved into a religious system during the Han dynasty (2nd century BCE onwards), it absorbed ancient Chinese beliefs about the soul. Every person was said to possess multiple souls—typically three heavenly souls (*hun*) and seven earthly souls (*po*).

The *hun* represent consciousness, intellect, and spiritual light; the *po* embody instinct, sensation, and attachment to the body. At death, the *hun* ascends to the heavens while the *po* returns to the earth. Depending on virtue, energy, and ritual observance, the hun may rise among the stars, linger in ancestral shrines, or descend again into the realm of the living.

This cosmology comes closer to reincarnation, but it differs in spirit. The returning soul is not an immutable self journeying through karmic recompense, but a current of life-force temporarily gathered into new form. The cycle is not moral accounting but the Dao's endless recycling of vitality.

The Search for Immortality

A distinctively Daoist response to death is the quest for immortality (*xian*). From the early centuries of the Common Era, adepts sought to prolong life and eventually transcend it altogether. Through meditation, breath control, inner alchemy, and herbal elixirs, they aimed to refine the body's *qi* into a purer spiritual substance that would survive beyond decay.

For the alchemist, reincarnation was a lesser path; true mastery meant freedom from the cycle altogether. The accomplished sage would "shed the corpse" and ascend to the heavens in a blaze of golden light. Whether interpreted literally or symbolically, this ideal of immortality represented harmony carried to perfection—the complete alignment of human and cosmic rhythms.

> "Those who follow the Way do not fear death;
> when life is full, they return to the root."
> — *Dao De Jing* 16

Even in this striving for longevity, the goal was not possession but participation: to live so naturally, so spontaneously, that one's life blended indistinguishably with the life of the universe.

Judgment and Return

By the Tang dynasty (7th–9th centuries CE), Daoism had absorbed Buddhist and folk influences. The heavens and hells of popular religion became elaborate bureaucracies presided over by the Ten Kings of the Underworld, who weighed each soul's deeds. Souls judged pure ascended to celestial realms; those burdened by wrongdoing were purified through various states of penance before being reborn.

Here the Indian notion of *karma* entered Chinese cosmology, translated through Daoist imagery of balance and natural law. Yet the metaphysical foundation remained Daoist: rebirth was not a moral ledger so much as restoration of harmony. Disorder created by human folly was rectified through cycles of change until equilibrium returned.

To the Daoist mind, the universe itself is moral in the deepest sense—not by decree but by design. Everything seeks balance, as water finds its level. Birth and death, gain and loss, are ripples on this self-correcting ocean.

Mystical Rebirth

The more contemplative branches of Daoism speak of spiritual rebirth within a single life. Meditation and inner alchemy aim to reverse the downward flow of energy and "return to the origin." This process, known as *neidan* (inner elixir cultivation), mirrors the cosmic creation in reverse: the adept gathers dispersed energies, refines them into spirit, and unites that spirit with the void.

The practitioner thus experiences multiple "deaths" and "births"—of ignorance into awareness, of form into formlessness. As in Sufism and Buddhism, reincarnation becomes a metaphor for awakening. Each moment of balance regained is a small resurrection.

> "Returning is the motion of the Dao.
> Weakness is the function of the Dao."
>
> — *Dao De Jing* 40

To return, in this sense, is not to repeat but to realise that all motion is circular and all opposites complete each other.

Life, Death, and the Flow of the Dao

Daoist death rituals express this continuity with gentle pragmatism. The dead are honoured not as vanished beings but as ancestors who have joined the greater rhythm of nature. Offerings of food, incense, and paper effigies sustain harmony between visible and invisible worlds. The boundary between the living and the dead is porous; the ancestors are still part of the family's *qi*.

This perspective fosters acceptance rather than anxiety. The goal is not to conquer death but to harmonise with it. As one text says, "The sage regards life as a loan, and death as the repayment." When the debt is paid, the spirit flows onward—not as a traveller carrying identity, but as water returning to the sea.

Reflection

Daoism's genius lies in its refusal to treat life and death as opposites. Instead of doctrines of salvation or judgment, it offers the quiet confidence of the natural world: that the cycle of transformation is itself divine. If there is reincarnation in Daoism, it is the reincarnation of energy—the endless arising and dissolving of forms within the great breathing of the cosmos.

Where Hinduism seeks liberation from the wheel of rebirth, and Buddhism the cessation of craving, Daoism finds freedom within the wheel—by recognising that it was never bondage at all. Everything is the Dao expressing itself; to resist is illusion, to flow is enlightenment.

> "Between heaven and earth it is like a bellows:
> empty, yet inexhaustible.
> The more it moves, the more it yields."
>
> — *Dao De Jing* 5

In that inexhaustible movement, the soul has no beginning and no end—only transformation. The sage, seeing this, smiles at death as at the turning of a season, knowing that the Way continues, forever renewing itself through all things.

SHINTO: THE WAY OF THE KAMI

ORIGIN	JAPAN, PREHISTORIC ROOTS, FORMALISED 8TH CENTURY CE
CORE SOURCES	KOJIKI; NIHON SHOKI
CENTRAL TEACHING	LIFE AS PARTICIPATION IN A LIVING WORLD OF KAMI
KEY THEMES	PURITY, GRATITUDE, HARMONY WITH NATURE AND ANCESTORS

Shinto, Japan's indigenous tradition, is often called "The Way of the *Kami*." Yet like the Dao, it is less a religion of doctrine than a living relationship with the world. The word *Shintō* (神道) combines shin—"divine, sacred"—and tō—"way, path." It points to a reverent way of being amid the ceaseless interplay of heaven, earth, and humanity.

Long before the arrival of Buddhism and Confucian ethics, the ancient Japanese felt the world to be alive with presence. Mountains, rivers, storms, trees, and ancestors all possessed kami—mysterious powers or spirits that animate and connect all things. The world was not divided between sacred and profane; rather, all life shimmered with sanctity. Shinto developed as the natural expression of that worldview—a tapestry of rituals, festivals, and acts of purification that sustain harmony between people and the unseen forces around them.

LIFE IN A LIVING WORLD

In Shinto thought, purity and pollution are not moral categories but conditions of energy. Purity (*harae*) means alignment with the natural flow of life; impurity (*kegare*) is a state of imbalance—the stagnation that follows grief, disease, or wrongdoing. The purpose of ritual is to restore freshness. Water is central: washing hands and mouth before entering a shrine symbolises the renewal of heart and spirit.

Death, too, is regarded as a form of impurity, not evil but disruptive of harmony. Traditionally, those involved in handling corpses or burial were ritually isolated until purification was completed. This sensitivity does not reflect fear of ghosts so much as a recognition that death changes the vibration of life—it needs to be acknowledged and balanced.

Because purity is constantly lost and regained, existence is understood as cyclical. The seasons, the harvests, the rhythms of work and celebration all enact the eternal renewal of life. The Shinto year is punctuated by festivals (*matsuri*)—communal acts of gratitude and communion with the kami. Through song, dance, and offering, human beings renew their covenant with the world that sustains them.

The Presence of Ancestors

For the Japanese, continuity lies not in reincarnation but in ancestral presence. The spirits of the dead are believed to watch over their descendants, receiving offerings of food, light, and remembrance. Families maintain *kamidana* (household altars) and *butsudan* (ancestral shrines) where incense is lit, prayers whispered, and the departed invited to share in daily life. During the midsummer festival of Obon, lanterns are set afloat on rivers and seas to guide the ancestors home, then back again to the spirit world—a graceful enactment of the flow between visible and invisible.

This relationship is reciprocal: the living care for the dead, and the dead bless the living. The boundary between life and death, like that between human and nature, is porous. To honour one's ancestors is to affirm that no life truly vanishes; it changes form and returns in spirit.

Death and Renewal

Shinto does not offer a detailed metaphysics of the afterlife. The earliest chronicles, the Kojiki (Records of Ancient Matters, 712 CE) and Nihon Shoki (Chronicles of Japan, 720 CE), tell of gods who die, descend to the shadowy realm of Yomi, and re-emerge transformed. These myths suggest that death is part of the creative rhythm of the cosmos. The world itself was born through separation—heaven from earth, light from darkness—and continues through the dance of loss and regeneration.

For most of Japanese history, Shinto and Buddhism have coexisted harmoniously, blending the Buddhist idea of rebirth with Shinto's focus on purity and gratitude. In everyday practice, a Japanese funeral is Buddhist, while a wedding or festival is Shinto. Thus, without formally teaching reincarnation, Shinto absorbs its emotional resonance: the sense that life renews itself endlessly and that the ancestors remain close.

> "As autumn dew that gleams a moment on the grass, so do our lives shine briefly and are gone."
> — *Man'yōshū* (8th-century Japanese anthology)

Nature as Continuum

If Hinduism finds the divine within the self and Buddhism in awareness, Shinto finds it in place—the sacredness of this mountain, this grove, this spring. Every locality has its guardian kami; every tree that lives long enough becomes a shrine. To stand before a *torii* gate—the red arch marking the boundary between ordinary space and sacred ground—is to pause at the threshold between seen and unseen, human and divine.

This sense of continuity with nature implicitly affirms rebirth, not as migration of souls but as perpetual renewal of form. The cherry blossom, symbol of impermanence, expresses it perfectly: beauty lies in transience. The petals fall, and new blossoms return each spring. Life's fragility is the very proof of its endurance.

Reflection

Shinto's vision of life after death is gentle and immanent. It does not ask where the soul goes but how harmony can be maintained between worlds. There is no dogma of heaven or hell, no final judgment—only the ongoing task of gratitude, purity, and celebration. Death is the winter of life's cycle, necessary for the coming of spring.

Where other traditions seek liberation from rebirth, Shinto finds holiness in recurrence itself. To live in tune with the seasons, to bow before the mountains, to remember one's ancestors with humility—this is salvation enough. Life is the ritual, and the world is the shrine.

> "Though the body fades, the heart returns,
> riding the wind that moves the grass."
> — *Manyōshū* (8th century anthology)

In the rhythm of Shinto, the universe is always beginning again. Every dawn, every festival, every breath is rebirth—the dance of the kami endlessly renewing the world.

YORUBA TRADITION: THE LIVING COSMOS

ORIGIN	YORUBA PEOPLES OF NIGERIA, BENIN, TOGO
CORE SOURCES	IFÁ CORPUS (VERSES OF ORUNMILA)
CENTRAL TEACHING	ATÚNWÁ: RETURN WITHIN FAMILY LINEAGE FO CONTINUED UNFOLDING
KEY THEMES	ORISHAS AS EXPRESSIONS OF THE DIVINE; INTERPLAY OF FATE (AYANMÓ) AND CHOICE

ACROSS WEST AFRICA, THE YORUBA PEOPLE OF NIGERIA, BENIN, AND Togo developed one of the world's most intricate and philosophically sophisticated spiritual systems. Long before contact with Islam or Christianity, they spoke of a universe both visible and invisible, woven together by divine intelligence. At its centre stands *Olódùmarè*, the Supreme Being—creator of all that is, distant yet immanent in every aspect of creation.

Between *Olódùmarè* and humanity moves a vast company of *Òrìṣà*—divine forces or deified ancestors who personify the laws of nature and the virtues of character. There is *Òṣun*, goddess of the river and fertility; *Ṣàngó*, spirit of thunder and justice; *Obàtálá*, the shaper of form; *Èṣù*, the messenger and guardian of crossroads. These powers are not idols but aspects of divine energy, accessible through ritual, prayer, and sacrifice. To live rightly is to stay in balance with the *Òrìṣà* and with one's destiny.

Destiny and the Soul (Orí)

Every human being, say the Yoruba, is born with an *ori*—literally "head," but spiritually one's inner self, personal destiny, and divine spark. Before birth, each soul kneels before *Olódùmarè* and chooses its *ayanmó*—the pattern of its life. Once incarnated, the soul forgets this choice, and the task of living is to remember and fulfil it.

The *Orí* is thus both guide and witness. When life goes astray, rituals of cleansing, divination, and offering realign the individual with the path they selected before birth. In this worldview, reincarnation is not a foreign idea but a natural expression of the soul's endurance. Life and death are complementary phases in the unfolding of *ori*—the same divine purpose continuing through different bodies and generations.

> "Destiny is a horse; if destiny agrees, blessings will come."
> — *Yoruba Proverb.*[1]

Ancestral Return (Atúnwá)

The Yoruba call reincarnation *atúnwá*, literally "coming back again." Yet it is not understood as a universal cycle of rebirth but as ancestral return within the family line. The departed who lived virtuously may choose to return among their descendants, often identified through birthmarks, character traits, or intuitive recognition. Such children are called *abíkú* ("born to die and be born again") or *babatúndé* ("father returns") and *yétúndé* ("mother returns").

This is not the migration of an isolated ego but the continuation of lineage—the ancestors renewing themselves through their own blood. The community participates in this continuity through naming ceremonies,

---

[1] *Owomoyela, Yoruba Proverbs,* University of Nebraska Press (2005)

songs, and storytelling that bind past and present. Death is therefore never final; it is a change of address within the family of existence.

> "The dead do not sleep; they are in the other world."
> — Traditional Yoruba funeral proverb,[2]

Ancestor veneration is central to Yoruba religious life. The living and the dead maintain a reciprocal relationship: the living honour the ancestors through prayer, libation, and moral conduct; the ancestors protect and guide the living through dreams, intuition, and circumstance. Forgetfulness is spiritual danger—to be forgotten is to fade from the web of life.

Festivals such as the *Egúngún* masquerades make this connection visible. During these ceremonies, dancers wearing elaborate costumes embody ancestral spirits who return to bless the community. The boundary between the worlds dissolves; the ancestors speak again through familiar voices. In this sense, reincarnation is not abstract theory but seasonal experience—renewal enacted in ritual time.

Life, Death, and the Journey of the Soul

At death, the soul (*emi*) leaves the body but not the world. It journeys to Òrun, the spiritual realm, where it rests, receives judgment, and may choose to return. The moral law of the universe, called ìwà (character), governs this process: those of good character enjoy peace and influence among the ancestors; those who neglect virtue remain restless. Yet even they are not condemned eternally—through the mercy of Olódùmarè and the prayers of the living, they may one day find renewal.

---

[2] cited in J. O. Lucas, *Religion in West Africa* (1948) The Cycle of Offerings and Memory

The afterlife in Yoruba cosmology is therefore dynamic, not static. Heaven and earth continually exchange energy; the ancestors are both memory and presence. The living prepare their own spiritual future by cultivating ìwà-pẹ̀ lẹ́ —gentle, balanced character—for "good character is the beauty of a person," and character endures beyond death.

REFLECTION

The Yoruba worldview unites the personal, the communal, and the cosmic in one continuous field of meaning. Reincarnation is not a doctrine of escape or punishment but an affirmation of relationship—the truth that life never travels alone. Each birth renews a covenant between ancestors and descendants, between the visible and the invisible, between GOD and creation.

Where Hinduism speaks of liberation from rebirth and Christianity of resurrection at the end of time, Yoruba wisdom finds holiness in continuity itself. The ancestors live on in their children, and the children carry the memory of their elders in their blood. Life is a single family gathering in many generations.

> "Understanding is the true prayer; the one who has understanding is answered."
> — YORUBA PROVERB, OWOMOYELA (2005)

To live with that awareness is to know that nothing truly dies—it only returns in another rhythm of the same divine dance.

AKAN TRADITION: THE BREATH OF *NYAME*

ORIGIN	AKAN PEOPLES OF GHANA & IVORY COAST
CORE SOURCES	ORAL TEACHINGS, PROVERBS, AND RITUAL KNOWLEDGE
CENTRAL TEACHING	THE SOUL (OKRA) RETURNS FOR MORAL AND COMMUNAL GROWTH
KEY THEMES	REVERENCE FOR *NYAME*; BALANCE, HARMONY, AND ETHICAL RESPONSIBILITY

AMONG THE AKAN PEOPLES OF WEST AFRICA—THE ASHANTI, Fante, Akyem, and others—religion is not a separate system but the fabric of life itself. The universe is filled with *Nyame*, the Supreme Being, whose name means "He who shines" or "He who is there." *Nyame* is transcendent yet intimate, manifest in sun, rain, and fertile earth. Through *Nyame's* breath every creature lives, and to *Nyame* every soul returns.

Beneath this highest divinity stands a network of *abosom*—deities or spirits associated with rivers, forests, and ancestors. They act as intermediaries between humans and *Nyame*, sustaining harmony in creation. The Akan world is therefore relational: each being depends on others, and every life is a thread in the continuous weaving of spirit and matter.

THE STRUCTURE OF THE PERSON

Akan anthropology distinguishes several components of the self, each participating in the rhythm of birth and death:

OKRA—the divine soul or life-essence, a spark of *Nyame* breathed into each person. It is pure, indestructible, and carries one's destiny (*nkrabea*).

SUNSUM—the personal spirit or character that develops through experience; it shapes and is shaped by moral choice.

HONAM—the physical body, fashioned from the earth and returning to it.

At birth, these elements unite; at death, they separate. The *honam* decays, the *sunsum* lingers with the family as ancestral presence, and the *okra* returns to *Nyame* for renewal. From that renewal arises the possibility of rebirth.

Reincarnation and Ancestral Return

The Akan speak of *nsamanfo*—the "living-dead," ancestors who continue to influence their descendants. A virtuous ancestor may be reborn within the same family line, recognised by traits of appearance, temperament, or instinctive behaviour. This process is known as rebirth through the lineage, not through anonymous cosmic cycles. The individual who returns is not an isolated ego but a continuation of ancestral spirit, resuming participation in family life.

Newborns are often observed for resemblances to departed elders, and names may acknowledge these recognitions: *Ama Nyameba* ("child of GOD"), *Nana Yaa* ("grandmother *Yaa* returns"). Diviners confirm such identities through ritual. The continuity is moral as well as biological—the ancestor's virtues and unfinished duties re-enter the world through the child.

> The life of the ancestors continues in their descendants."
> — *AKAN PROVERB, KOFI AGYEKUM.*[3]

---

[3] *Akan Proverbs: The Aesthetics and Functions of Akan Proverbs* (University of Ghana)

The Moral Law (Nkrabea and Sunsum)

Each soul carries its *nkrabea*, the divine purpose chosen before birth. Life's task is to realise that destiny through right character (*suban pa*). Actions contrary to destiny create imbalance, bringing misfortune or illness; moral living restores harmony. The soul's progress through successive lives is not punishment but education—the gradual ripening of sunsum until it mirrors the purity of *okra*.

Because the community shares spiritual substance, moral failure injures not only the individual but the lineage. Hence the Akan stress communal ethics: honesty, generosity, respect for elders, and care for the poor. Through virtue, one becomes a "complete person" (*onipa pa*), preparing for peaceful return to the ancestors and, perhaps, rebirth among them.

Death, Funerals, and the Journey Home

Death, for the Akan, is a transition, not an end. The funeral is both solemn and festive—mourning for the loss and celebration of the return. Drumming, dancing, and praise poetry accompany the soul on its way to the ancestral village. Offerings of food, drink, and cloth express continuity between the visible and invisible worlds. For forty days after death, the *sunsum* lingers near home, listening to the prayers of the living before departing fully to join the *nsamanfo*.

The ancestors remain guardians of morality. Their blessing is invoked before major undertakings; their displeasure is feared when taboos are broken. Through ritual libation, the living acknowledge that they stand on the shoulders of those who came before. Forgetting the ancestors severs the chain of blessing; remembering them renews life's sacred flow.

The Wider Vision

Reincarnation in Akan thought is therefore familial, moral, and cyclical, but not infinite. Souls return until their purpose is fulfilled and their character perfected. When a spirit's learning is complete, its okra rests permanently with *Nyame*, absorbed into divine peace. Thus the cycle is not endless repetition but spiritual maturation.

The living world and the ancestral world interpenetrate like day and night; each gives birth to the other. Children embody the hope of the dead, and the dead embody the wisdom of the living. Time, in this cosmology, is a spiral: what seems to end always curves back toward its beginning.

> "The ancestors are also the living."
> — *Akan Proverb, Rattray* (1923)

Reflection

The Akan tradition transforms reincarnation from a theory of metaphysics into a practice of memory. To be reborn is not merely to live again, but to continue the moral work of the family and the cosmos. The soul's journey is measured in character, not in years. When one acts with integrity and compassion, one's life already joins the ancestors; when one is born with their virtues, one continues their song.

Where Indian faiths trace liberation through detachment and Western faiths through salvation, Akan wisdom locates immortality in belonging. The self endures by remaining part of the community's heartbeat—each life a verse in the same ancestral hymn.

> "No one knows the beginning of a great person."
> — *Akan Proverb, Agyekum* (2012)

In that recognition lies a serene confidence: that the thread of being is unbroken, and that through every birth and death, *Nyame's* breath continues to move in the world.

You Again

GRECO-ROMAN & PLATONIC TRADITIONS

Origin	Greece & Rome (6th century BCE onward)
Core Sources	Plato's *Phaedo* & *Republic* (Book X); Virgil's *Aeneid* (Book VI); Plotinus' *Enneads*
Central Teaching	Immortality of the soul and moral purification across lifetimes
Key Themes	Philosophy as soul-education; cosmic justice; ascent toward virtue

THE WESTERN IMAGINATION FIRST ENCOUNTERED THE IDEA OF reincarnation not through religion but through philosophy. In the sixth century BCE, the Greek sage Pythagoras taught that the soul is immortal and migrates from one body to another in an endless education. "All things are akin," he said, and the wise abstain from violence because one never knows in what form a soul may appear. The Pythagoreans saw life as a discipline of purification (*katharsis*): through harmony, music, mathematics, and virtue, the soul frees itself from the coarse vibrations of matter and ascends toward the divine order of number.

From these beginnings grew a distinct Western vision of transmigration—part mystical, part rational—that would echo for more than a millennium. The soul's return was not punishment but pedagogy, the schooling of consciousness through many experiences until it remembered its origin.

Plato and the Education of the Soul

Two centuries later, Plato gave the doctrine its most influential form. In the *Phaedo*, he presents Socrates on the eve of his death, serene in the conviction that the philosopher merely goes "from men to gods." The soul, he argues, is eternal and indestructible: it comes from a world of pure forms and returns there when liberated from the body's distractions. Those who cling to bodily pleasures are reborn in lower states; those who cultivate virtue ascend toward truth.

Plato's mythic accounts describe this in vivid allegory. In the *Republic's Myth of Er*, a soldier slain in battle is allowed to witness the machinery of destiny: souls choosing their next lives, guided by the *Fates*, drinking from the river of forgetfulness before returning to earth. In the *Phaedrus*, souls are likened to winged chariots circling the heavens; through neglect they fall into matter, through wisdom they regain their wings.

> "The soul is immortal, for that which moves itself never ceases to move."
>
> — *Phaedrus* 245c

For Plato, then, reincarnation served a moral purpose. Knowledge is remembrance (*anamnesis*)—learning is the soul's recollection of truths once known. Each life offers another chance to recover that memory.

From Philosophy to Mystery

As Greek thought met Eastern and Egyptian traditions, the idea of rebirth intertwined with mystery religions—Orphic, Dionysian, and later Roman cults that promised purification and renewal beyond death. The Orphic tablets buried with initiates bear short inscriptions such as: "I am a child of Earth and of starry Heaven, but my race is of Heaven alone." These words reflect the ancient yearning to escape the cycle of mortality through divine remembrance.

Roman thinkers absorbed these ideas with characteristic pragmatism. Cicero accepted the soul's immortality but treated reincarnation metaphorically—as the return of influence and virtue through history. Virgil's *Aeneid* imagines souls waiting by the *River Lethe* to be reborn into new bodies, hinting that even the empire itself participates in cosmic renewal.

The Stoics and the Eternal Return

The Stoic philosophers, beginning with Zeno and Chrysippus, rejected the notion of individual reincarnation but affirmed a grander rhythm: the eternal return of the cosmos itself. They taught that the universe periodically dissolves in fire (*ekpyrosis*) and is reborn exactly as before—every event repeating in infinite cycles. In this deterministic vision, each soul participates in nature's rational order (*logos*), playing its role again and again across endless worlds.

Later thinkers softened this severity. For Marcus Aurelius, rebirth was not literal but psychological: each dawn is a new beginning, each moment an opportunity to act in harmony with reason. "Frequently consider the connection of all things," he wrote. "What is born of earth returns to earth; what springs from heaven returns to heaven."

Neoplatonism and the Return to the ONE

In the third century CE, Plotinus, founder of Neoplatonism, gathered these streams into a single vision of emanation and return. All reality flows from the ineffable ONE, through the levels of *Nous* (Divine Mind) and *Psyche* (World-Soul), into the multiplicity of matter. The human soul, a spark of that World-Soul, descends into embodiment to gain experience and knowledge, then rises again through contemplation and virtue. If its desire for the material binds it, it may descend once more into new forms—human, animal, or celestial—until it realises its true unity with the divine.

"Never stop sculpting your own statue," Plotinus wrote.

"Cut away what is superfluous; make it perfect until the godlike splendour of virtue shines forth."

Rebirth, in this context, is refinement—the slow polishing of the soul's mirror until it reflects the ONE perfectly.

The Twilight of the Ancient World

By the time Christianity became dominant in the late Roman Empire, these ideas of the soul's migration had shaped centuries of philosophical and poetic imagination. Early Christian theologians such as Origen and Gregory of Nyssa preserved elements of this Platonic heritage, proposing that souls existed before birth and might return until fully restored in GOD. Later orthodoxy rejected such speculation, but the Platonic myth of descent and return continued to haunt Western thought, resurfacing in Renaissance humanism and Romantic mysticism.

Reflection

In the classical world, reincarnation was never a creed imposed by authority; it was a metaphor for moral continuity and cosmic order. Whether in Plato's myths, the Orphic hymns, or the meditations of Stoic emperors, the same intuition recurs: the soul is not extinguished but educated by time. Each birth is an opportunity to remember what the soul already knows—that its true home lies beyond the transient forms it inhabits.

Where the Eastern traditions speak of *karma* and liberation, the Greeks spoke of *virtue* and *recollection*; where others sought to escape the cycle, Plato urged us to perfect it through wisdom. The ancient philosophers thus offered the West its own language of return—the idea that through learning, love, and contemplation, the soul may ascend again to the light from which it came.

> "The life of man is a pilgrimage of the soul.
> From the gods we come, to the gods we shall return."
> — *Traditional Hellenic maxim*

You Again

NORSE & CELTIC TRADITIONS

ORIGIN	NORTHERN & WESTERN EUROPE (SCANDINAVIA, THE BRITISH ISLES, GAUL; C. 1000 BCE–800 CE)
CORE SOURCES	POETIC EDDA, PROSE EDDA; CELTIC CYCLES SUCH AS *THE MABINOGION* AND *BOOK OF INVASIONS*
CENTRAL TEACHING	TIME AS CYCLICAL; RETURN THROUGH ANCESTRY, CLAN, AND FATE
KEY THEMES	WYRD (WOVEN DESTINY); REVERENCE FOR NATURE AND ANCESTORS; HEROIC VIRTUE

ACROSS THE FORESTS AND SEAWAYS OF EARLY EUROPE, LONG BEFORE Christianity took root, people lived with a profound sense of continuity between the worlds of the living and the dead. The Norse of Scandinavia and the Celts of Ireland, Scotland, and Gaul each imagined existence as a circle rather than a line—a rhythm of death and renewal in which ancestors and descendants shared one enduring life.

Both traditions lacked a single sacred text, but their poetry and myth echo a shared intuition: the spirit does not vanish; it returns in kin, in story, or in the natural world itself. Memory, lineage, and the eternal return of the seasons were the Western echoes of reincarnation.

THE NORSE: *WYRD* AND RETURN

The Norse cosmos was woven from fate (*wyrd* or *urðr*)—an interlocking pattern of causes traced by the Norns, the goddesses who spin the threads of life beneath Yggdrasil, the World Tree. All beings, even the gods, are bound by this web of destiny. Death, therefore, is not extinction but a change of thread: the pattern continues, re-woven into new forms.

Ancestral Rebirth

Several Old Norse sources suggest belief in rebirth within the family line, particularly among heroes and chieftains. The *Íslendingabók* and *Landnámabók* (Icelandic genealogies) record names passed down through generations with explicit claims of the soul's return. The custom of naming a newborn after a deceased relative—often a grandparent—was not mere honour; it was a recognition of identity reborn. Medieval sagas tell of seers predicting that a child carries the spirit of an ancestor, a belief known as *hamingja* (fortune or spiritual power).

To inherit someone's *hamingja* was to inherit their luck, courage, and fate—an echo of reincarnation through lineage. In the *Saga of Helgi and Sigrun*, the lovers Helgi and Sigrun are reborn as Helgi Haddingjaskati and Kara, resuming their bond in another life. The poem closes with the line:

> "It is said that Helgi and Kara were born again."
> (*Helgakviða Hundingsbana II*, stanza 50)

This is among the clearest attestations of rebirth in the Old Norse corpus.

The Afterlife of Heroes

Norse cosmology also describes multiple afterlives: Valhalla for warriors, Fólkvangr for those chosen by *Freyja, Hel* for ordinary souls, and the unknown seas beyond. Yet even these realms are not final. At *Ragnarök*, the world's end and rebirth, the dead return: *Baldr*, the slain god of light, comes back from *Hel* to rule the renewed earth. Thus, even the gods participate in the cycle of destruction and renewal.

Rebirth in the Norse imagination is cosmic and heroic—the return of divine forces through the ages, mirrored in the human practice of ancestral naming and the endurance of family fate.

THE CELTS: THE EVER-LIVING ONES

Among the ancient Celts, reincarnation appears even more explicitly. Classical authors who encountered the Druids—notably Julius Caesar, Lucan, and Diodorus Siculus—consistently record that they taught the transmigration of souls. Caesar wrote in *De Bello Gallico* (Book VI):

> "The Druids strive to inculcate this belief, that souls do not perish, but after death pass from one body to another; by this doctrine they think that men are much encouraged to valour, since the fear of death is disregarded."

This statement, corroborated by other Roman observers, shows that *Metempsychōsis* was central to Druidic philosophy, not a marginal belief. The Celts saw death as a threshold, not an ending.

THE WORLD OF THE *SÍDHE*

In Irish myth, the boundary between life and death is porous. Heroes such as Cúchulainn and Fionn mac Cumhaill move easily between worlds; the Tuatha Dé Danann, divine ancestors of the Irish, retreat into the hollow hills and become the immortal *Aes Sídhe*—"People of the Mounds." The *sídhe* are not ghosts but transformed beings, their rebirth occurring in subtler realms.

Later tales describe human souls returning to earthly life. The Mabinogion and Lebor Gabála Érenn speak of heroes reborn across epochs, carrying memory or destiny from one age to the next. The poet Taliesin in medieval Welsh tradition recounts his own many lives:

> "I have been a drop in the air,
> I have been a shining star,
> I have been a word in a book,
> I have been a harp-string resonant in the wind."
> (THE BATTLE OF THE TREES, CAD GODDEU)

This poem, though allegorical, captures the Celtic vision of the soul as shape-shifter—ever transforming, yet retaining a secret core of awareness.

CYCLES OF NATURE AND SPIRIT

Both Norse and Celtic cosmologies root human destiny in the rhythms of the natural world. Winter's death leads to spring's rebirth; crops, animals, and stars follow eternal cycles. The festivals of *Samhain* and *Beltane*, marking the hinge-points of the year, mirror this transformation. *Samhain* (the Celtic New Year) celebrates communion with ancestors, when the veil between worlds thins and souls revisit their homes—an annual return that reinforces belief in continuity.

In Norse Yule and the Celtic *Samhain* alike, fire rituals and feasting acknowledge the circle of loss and renewal: the sun dies and is reborn, echoing the soul's own passage through darkness back into light.

DEATH AND MEMORY

Funeral practices in both cultures reflect an expectation of ongoing life. The Norse buried the dead with weapons, food, and ships—provisions for another voyage. The Celts interred or cremated the body with grave goods, ornaments, and personal tokens, suggesting that identity endured beyond the grave. The persistence of grave offerings through centuries shows a sustained faith that the dead remained active members of the community.

For both peoples, memory was immortality. The bards and skalds ensured that the names of heroes lived on, their deeds sung into future generations. In the oral tradition, remembrance and reincarnation intertwine: to be remembered is to live again in word and story.

Reflection

The Norse and Celtic visions of afterlife combine courage with continuity. They accept mortality yet deny oblivion. Whether through the rebirth of heroes, the transmigration of Druids, or the cosmic renewal at the world's end, life is portrayed as an eternal rhythm: what has been will be again.

Where Eastern thought refined reincarnation into moral law, the northern mind expressed it as mythic recurrence—the turning of fate's wheel, the song that returns in a new verse. Every birth carries ancestral power; every death feeds the roots of future life.

> "Everything that is, will be again; the wave that falls rises once more."
>
> — PARAPHRASE OF HÁVAMÁL 153

To live bravely, then, was to join that rhythm knowingly—to die as one who returns, and to return as one who remembers. For the Norse and the Celts alike, eternity was not elsewhere; it was the endless renewal of the world they already loved.

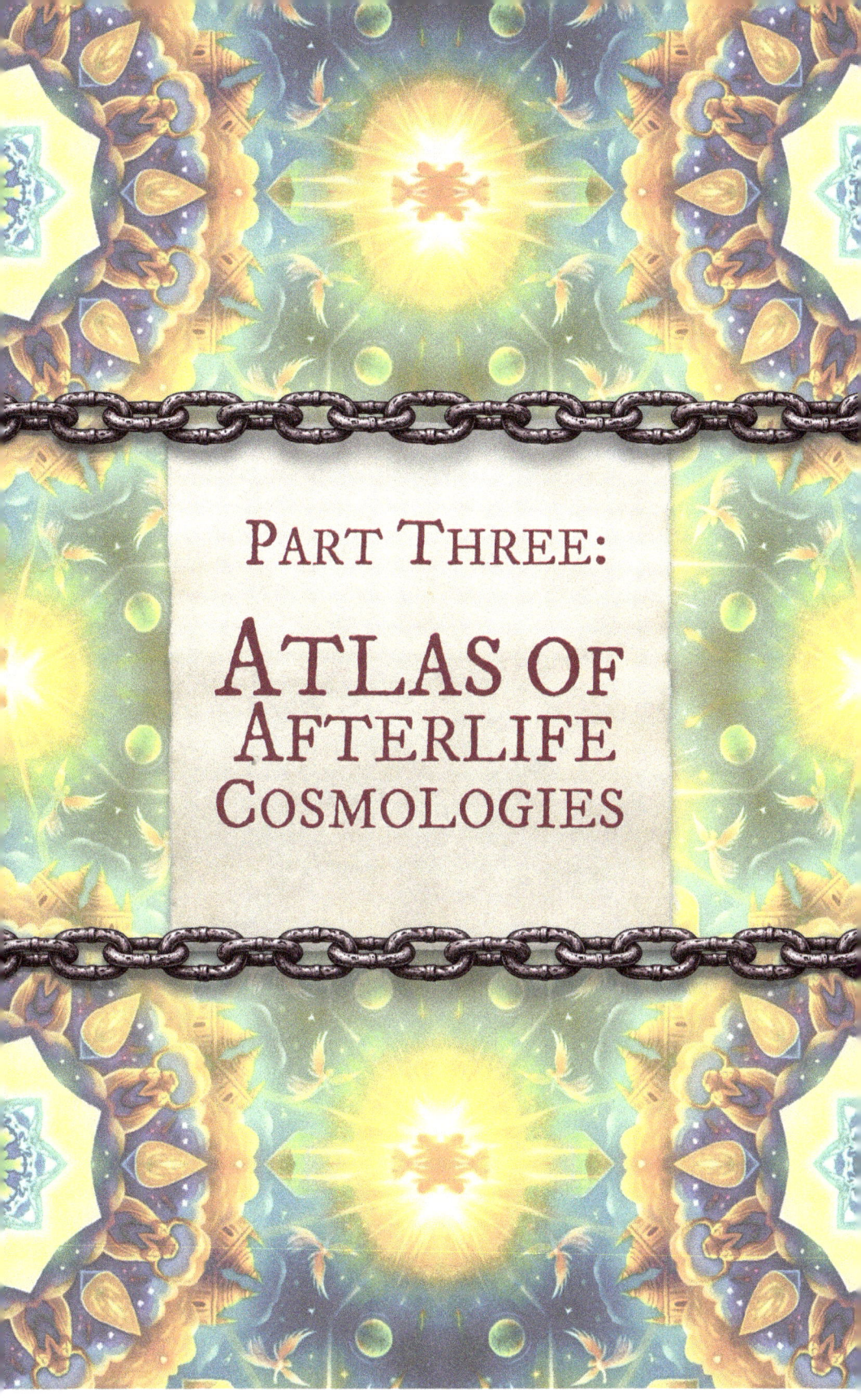

Part Three:
Atlas of Afterlife Cosmologies

Table: 1. The Anatomy of the Soul

Tradition	THE PASSENGER (*The Eternal Part*)	THE SHELL (*The Mortal Part*)	THE CARRIER (*The Vehicle*)
HINDUISM	ĀTMAN: The uncreated Self, identical to the Divine.	STHŪLA ŚARĪRA: The physical body that decays.	SŪKṢMA ŚARĪRA: The subtle body carrying karmic data.
BUDDHISM	CITTA-SANTANA: The "mind-stream" or causal continuum.	RŪPA: The physical form (AGGREGATES).	VIÑÑĀṆA: Consciousness conditioned by *karma*.
ANCIENT EGYPT	AKH: The transfigured spirit (union of *Ba* and *Ka*).	KHAT: The physical body (preserved by mummification).	BA: The personality-soul that travels between worlds.
DAOISM	HUN: The cloud-soul (*Yang*) that ascends to heaven.	PO: The white-bone soul (*Yin*) that stays with the corpse.	QI: The vital energy that disperses into nature.
JUDAISM (Kabbalah)	NESHAMAH: The divine breath/intellect.	GUF: The physical body.	RUACH: The emotional spirit that connects body and soul.
AKAN (Ghana)	OKRA: The soul carrying the destiny (*nkrabea*).	HONAM: The physical body.	SUNSUM: The personality/spirit that becomes an ancestor.

Atlas Of Afterlife Cosmologies

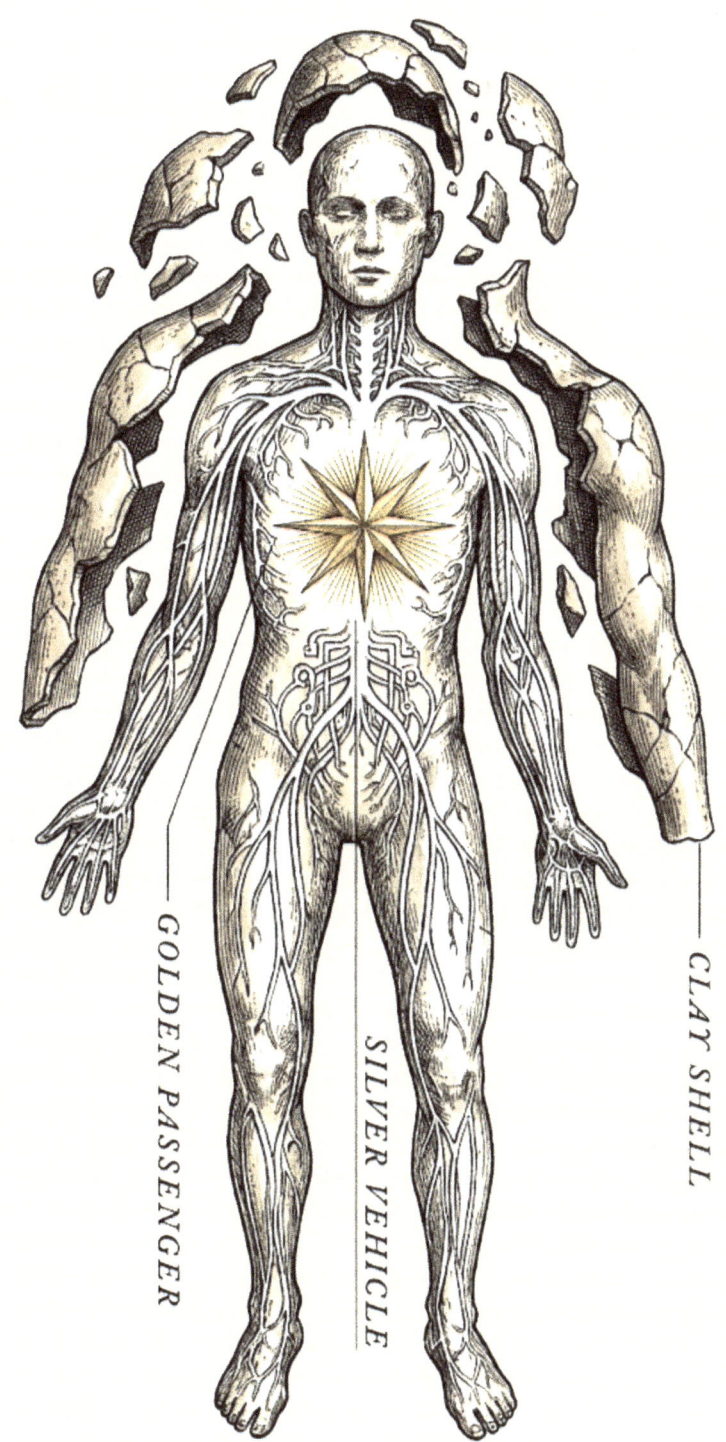

A Cartography of the Invisible

The human impulse to map the unknown is nowhere more fervent than in the domain of death. Across millennia, civilisations have refused to accept the cessation of biological function as the boundary of existence. Instead, they have constructed elaborate, highly structured cosmologies—veritable atlases of the invisible—to describe the trajectory of the vital principle after it severs ties with the physical body.

This Atlas treats the afterlife not as a vague "dream state," but as a geographical and mechanical reality governed by laws as rigorous as gravity or thermodynamics. Just as a medical text maps the circulatory system, this text maps the circulation of the soul.

To navigate this terrain, we categorise the major afterlife systems into three distinct "physics":

Type A: THE CYCLICAL COSMOS INDO-TIBETAN
Existence is a VERTICAL HIGH-RISE. The soul is an entity driven up or down by the specific gravity of *Karma*.

Type B: THE LINEAR-ASCENSION MODELS WESTERN/MONO-THEISTIC
Existence is a LADDER OR A REFINING FIRE. The soul is a spark returning to its Source through stages of purification.

Type C: THE ANCESTRAL CONTINUUM INDIGENOUS/EAST ASIAN
Existence is a PARALLEL DIMENSION. The dead do not leave; they become invisible elders in a reciprocal ecosystem with the living.

ATLAS OF AFTERLIFE COSMOLOGIES

TYPE A: THE CYCLICAL COSMOS

The universe is a wheel of cause and effect

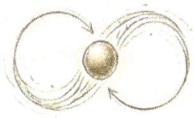

The soul is trapped in a continuous cycle of birth, death, and rebirth (Samsara).

The Engine is Karma
Moral actions create "weight," determining if a soul rises or sinks in the next life.

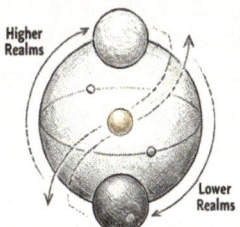

The Ultimate Goal is to EXIT the cycle
To achieve liberation (Moksha/Nirvana) and stop the process of rebirth entirely.

Geography: A vertical "high-rise" of realms.
Transition: An instantaneous transfer or a journey through an intermediate state (Bardo).
Examples: Hinduism, Buddhism, Jainism.

TYPE B: THE LINEAR-ASCENSION MODEL

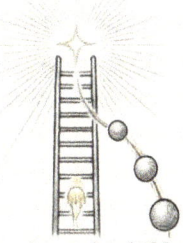

The universe is a ladder back to the Source

The soul is on a one-way journey of purification and return to a state of perfection.

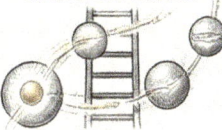

The Engine is Judgment
The soul's fate is decided by a moral text, divine decree, or rational choice.

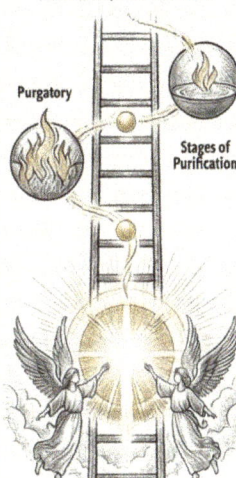

The Ultimate Goal is UNION with the divine
To ascend through purgatorial stages and be reunited with God or Ultimate Reality.

Geography: A ladder or refinery of spheres.
Transition: A long period of cleansing or judgment (Purgatory).
Examples: Christianity, Ancient Egypt, Sufism.

TYPE C: THE ANCESTRAL CONTINUUM

The afterlife is a parallel world, not a distant one

The dead do not leave; they become invisible members of the community.

The Engine is Reciprocity
A mutual duty exists between the living and the dead for protection and sustenance.

The Ultimate Goal is to MAINTAIN the lineage
To become a revered ancestor who ensures the continuity and prosperity of their family.

Geography: A parallel world next door.
Transition: A crossing over a boundary (e.g., a river that requires a raft).
Examples: Yoruba, Celtic, Shinto.

Type A: The Cyclical Cosmos

Core Principle:

CONSERVATION OF CONSCIOUSNESS. ENERGY IS NEVER DESTROYED, only transformed. The universe is a closed loop of cause and effect.

We begin in the East, where time is not a straight line but a turning wheel. Here, the afterlife is not a final destination but a transit lounge—a temporary state determined by the moral weight of one's actions. Whether called *Saṃsāra* or the Wheel of Becoming, the physics here are vertical: heavy souls sink, light souls rise, but all must eventually return, until the cycle itself is broken.

ATLAS OF AFTERLIFE COSMOLOGIES

HINDUISM: *The Fourteen-Fold Ladder of Being*

~ SYSTEM PROFILE ~

TYPE:	CYCLICAL / VERTICAL HIERARCHY
ENGINE:	*KARMA* (Action) & *SAMSKĀRA* (Subtle Impressions)
CORE PRINCIPLE:	CONSERVATION OF CONSCIOUSNESS. Energy is never destroyed, only transformed. The universe is a closed loop of moral cause and effect where the soul's destination is determined by its specific karmic gravity—heavy *karma* sinks, light *karma* rises.

~ ANATOMY OF THE TRAVELER ~

PASSENGER:	ĀTMAN. The indestructible, eternal core. It is uncreated, undying, stable, and identical in essence to BRAHMAN (Ultimate Reality). It is the silent witness to the journey.
SHELL:	STHŪLA ŚARĪRA (*The Physical Body*). The biological casing that decays at death.
CARRIER:	SŪKṢMA ŚARĪRA (*The Subtle Body*). A metaphysical chassis that survives the death of the physical body. It acts as a "data drive," carrying the load of *saṃskāras* (karmic imprints and unfulfilled desires) from one life to the next.
KEY METAPHOR:	THE CHANGING OF GARMENTS. "As a person sheds worn-out garments and puts on new ones, so the soul casts off a worn-out body and enters a new one." (*Bhagavad Gītā* 2.22).

~ CARTOGRAPHY OF THE INVISIBLE ~

HINDU cosmology posits a universe of staggering scale, often visualised as the *Viśvarūpa* (Cosmic Man) or a multi-dimensional high-rise consisting of 14 *Lokas* (Planetary Systems).

ATLAS OF AFTERLIFE COSMOLOGIES

Anatomy of the Traveler

The Eternal Passenger
(Atman)
The indestructible, uncreated, and undying soul. It is the silent witness to the journey, identical in essence to Brahman.

The Vehicle
(Sukshma Sharira)
A metaphysical chassis that survives death and carries the karmic imprints (samskaras) and unfulfilled desires.

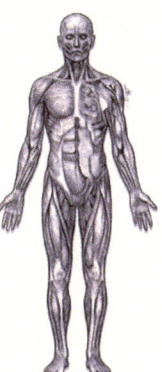

The Mortal Shell
(Sthula Sharira)
Physical Body
The biological casing that decays and is discarded at death.

"As a person sheds worn-out garments and puts on new ones, so the soul casts off a worn-out body and enters a new one."
- Bhagavad Gita 2.22

Upper Worlds
Satya, Tapa, Jana, Mahar
Abodes of Truth, Austerity, and Creative Generation high spiritual frequency and extended lifespans.

Svar-loka
Middle Heavens
In immense sensory pleasure. *Temporary Reward. Existence is temporary. When the credit of good merit is exhausted, the soul falls back to Earth.

Bhuvar-loka
Atmosphere
intermediate realm.
(Yakshas, Gandharvas)

Bhu-loka
The Earth

*The Field of Action (Karma Bhumi):
Only here can one change destiny. All other realms are for consuming the fruits of past action.

The Lower Worlds
Not hells, but realms of immense material opulence, technological wizardry, and sensual delight. Characterized by an absence of spiritual wisdom and obsession with power.

Naraka
The Penal Colony
A reformative prison ruled by Yama with specific hells designed to burn off heavy negative karma before the soul is recycled into a lower biological form.

The Cosmic Engine: Mechanics of Transition

Primary Engine:
Karma & Samsara
Cycle of actions and moral cause and effect... driven to act again by subtle impressions.

Karmic Gravity
Heavy attachments cause the soul to sink; righteous deeds lighten it, allowing it to rise.

Determines

The Moment of Death
The soul's trajectory is calculated by the state of mind at the precise moment of death, which is the cumulative result of lifelong habits and impressions.

Kama

The Cycle of Samsara
This automatic and continuous process is propelled by desire (*kama*), impelling the soul from a departing body into a compatible womb.

The Ultimate Goal: Liberation

Moksha: The "Win Condition"
Liberation is achieved by exiting the cycle of Samsara entirely. This happens when the Atman realizes it is distinct from the body and mind, and identical to the Divine.

Path to Attainment

Moksha is attained through Yoga (*Jnana* - Knowledge, *Bhakti* - Devotion, or *Karma* - Selfless Action).

~ The Mechanics of Transition ~

MOMENT OF DEATH:	The trajectory of the soul is calculated by the state of mind at the PRECISE MOMENT OF DEATH. However, this final thought is not random; it is the cumulative result of lifelong habits (saṃskāras).
KARMIC GRAVITY:	The mechanics are biological and physics-based, not punitive. Just as oil floats on water and stone sinks, a soul "weighted" by HEAVY ATTACHMENTS naturally sinks to lower wombs or realms, while a soul "lightened" by VIRTUE rises.
CYCLE (SAṂSĀRA):	The process is AUTOMATIC and CONTINUOUS. Upon leaving the body, the subtle body is propelled by the winds of desire (kama) into a compatible womb to continue its education.

~ The Ultimate Goal ~

MOKṢA:	LIBERATION. The "Win Condition" is to EXIT the cycle entirely.
ACHIEVED:	When the *ĀTMAN* realises it is distinct from the body and mind, and identical to the Divine.
ATTAINED:	Through YOGA: *Jhana* (Knowledge), *Bhakti* (Devotion), or *Karma* (Selfless Action).

From Substance to Process

While HINDUISM envisions a permanent traveler (the *ĀTMAN*) moving from body to body, the BUDDHA challenged the very existence of the *traveler*. If there is no permanent self, *what* is reborn? The following model retains the cyclic geography of India but subtracts the soul, replacing the "changing of clothes" with the transfer of a flame.

Table: 2. The Map of Hindu Realms

Realm Group	Specific Lokas	Description & Condition
The Upper Worlds (Realms of Light)	Satya, Tapa, Jana, Mahar	The abodes of Truth, Austerity, and Creative Generation. Inhabited by Brahma, ascetics (*tapasvis*), and seers (*rishis*). These are realms of high spiritual frequency and extended lifespans.
The Middle Heavens (Temporary Reward)	Svar-loka (Svarga)	The "Heaven" of the Devas (ruled by Indra). A realm of immense sensory pleasure. **Crucial Note:** Residence here is temporary. When the "credit" of good merit is exhausted, the soul falls back to Earth.
The Atmosphere	Bhuvar-loka	The intermediate realm, home to nature spirits, *Yakshas*, and *Gandharvas*.
The Earth	Bhu-loka	**The Field of Action (*Karma-bhumi*).** This is the only realm where *new karma* can be generated. All other realms are merely for consuming the fruits of past action. Only here can one change destiny.
The Lower Worlds (Subterranean Heavens)	Atala, Vitala, Sutala, Talatala, Mahatala, Rasatala, Patala	These are *not* hells, but realms of immense material opulence, technological wizardry, and sensual delight. Inhabited by *Asuras* (demons) and *Nagas*. Characterized by the absence of sunlight (spiritual wisdom) and an obsession with power.
The Penal Colony	Naraka	Distinct from the Lower Worlds. A reformative prison ruled by Yama (Lord of Justice). There are 28 specific hells (e.g., *Asipatravana*, the sword-leaf forest) designed to burn off heavy negative karma before the soul is recycled into a lower biological form.

CLASSICAL BUDDHISM (THERAVĀDA):
The Flame Without a Wick

~ SYSTEM PROFILE ~

TYPE:	CYCLICAL / CAUSAL CONTINUUM
ENGINE:	KARMA (*Action*) & CRAVING (*Taṇhā*)
CORE PRINCIPLE:	DEPENDENT ORIGINATION (*Paṭicca-samuppāda*). Existence is a CHAIN OF TWELVE LINKS where ignorance conditions consciousness, leading inevitably to birth and death. Rebirth is INSTANTANEOUS—one mind-moment conditioning the next—without a permanent soul.

~ ANATOMY OF THE TRAVELER ~

PASSENGER:	NONE (*Anattā*). There is no permanent self or soul. What continues is a CITTA-SANTĀNA ("Mind-Stream"), a causal continuum of consciousness carrying karmic imprints.
SHELL:	*Rūpa* (The PHYSICAL FORM/AGGREGATES). The body that decays at death.
CARRIER:	*Viññāṇa* (CONSCIOUSNESS). Specifically, the *Patisandhi-Citta* (*rebirth-linking consciousness*) which arises immediately after the DEATH-CONSCIOUSNESS of the previous life.
KEY METAPHOR:	THE FLAME TRANSFER. "The flame on the second candle is not the same flame as the first, nor is it different; it is causally connected."

~ CARTOGRAPHY OF THE INVISIBLE ~

The BUDDHIST cosmos is mapped as the Bhavachakra (Wheel of Life), divided into SIX DISTINCT REALMS OF EXISTENCE (*gati*), driven by the THREE POISONS at the hub: IGNORANCE (Pig), GREED (Rooster), and HATRED (Snake).

ATLAS OF AFTERLIFE COSMOLOGIES

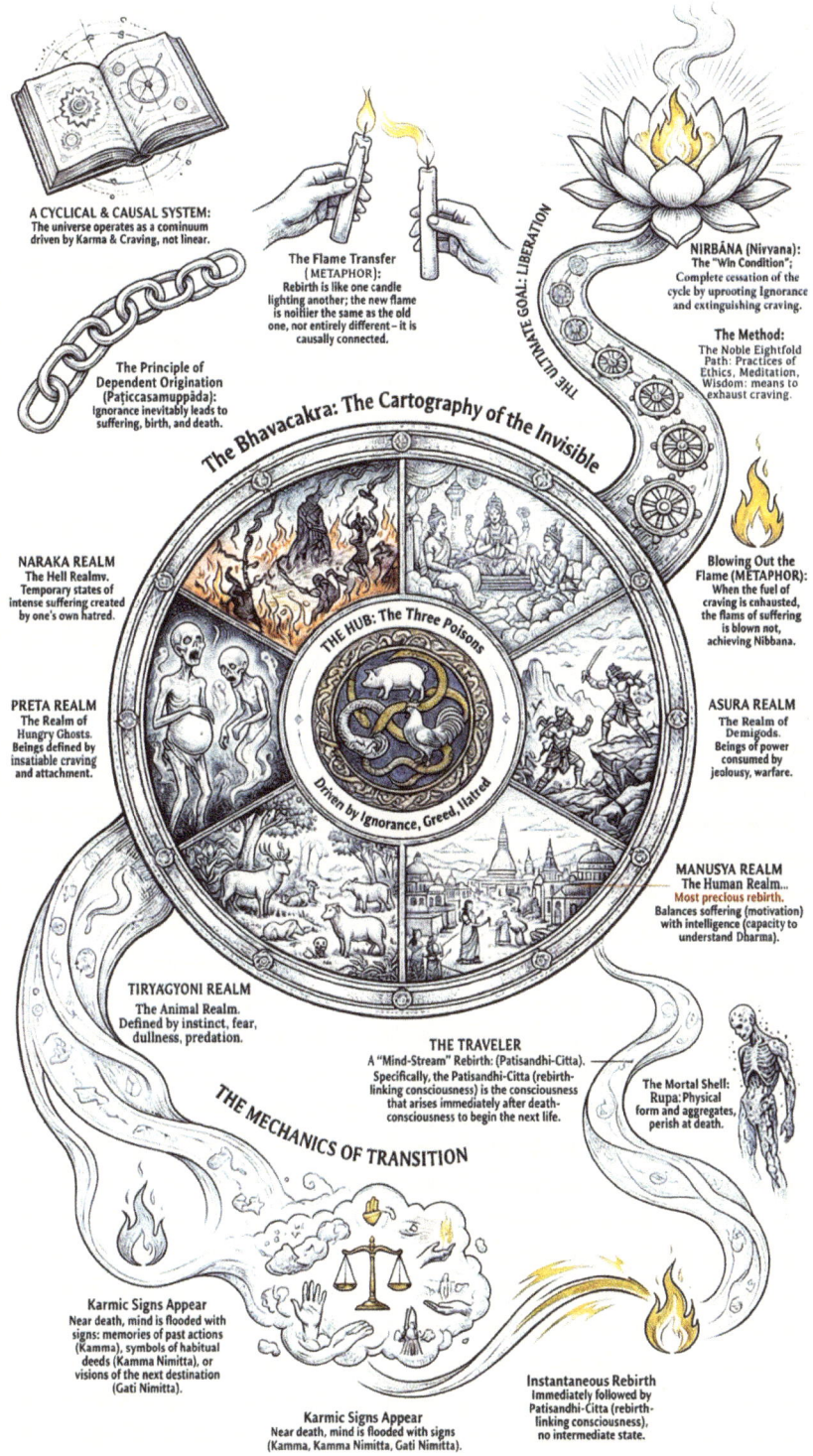

Table: 3. The Map of Buddhist Realms

Realm Name	Description	Inhabitants/Condition
Deva Realm	The Realm of Gods. A place of immense aesthetic pleasure and long life.	**Devas.** Dangerous due to complacency; when good *karma* is exhausted, the fall is painful.
Asura Realm	The Realm of Demigods. Beings of power consumed by jealousy and constant warfare against the Devas.	**Asuras.** Titans/Demigods driven by envy and conflict.
Manusya Realm	The Human Realm. The most precious rebirth. It balances suffering (motivation to escape) with intelligence (capacity to understand *Dharma*).	**Humans.** The only realm where enlightenment is readily accessible.
Tiryagyoni Realm	The Animal Realm. Defined by instinct, fear, dullness, and the predation of the strong upon the weak.	**Animals.** Driven by survival instincts and ignorance.
Preta Realm	The Realm of Hungry Ghosts. Beings defined by insatiable craving and attachment.	**Pretas.** Depicted with swollen bellies and needle-thin necks, unable to satisfy their hunger.
Naraka Realm	The Hell Realms. Temporary states of intense suffering (hot or cold) created by one's own hatred and violence.	**Hell Beings.** Tormented by their own karmic projections until the negative *karma* is exhausted.

~ The Mechanics of Transition ~

CUTI-CITTA: The FINAL MOMENT OF CONSCIOUSNESS in one life (death-consciousness). It acts as a condition for the immediate arising of the next moment.

INSTANTANEOUS: REBIRTH: Unlike models with an intermediate state (like the Tibetan *BARDO*), Theravāda posits an immediate transfer. The *Cuti-Citta* is followed instantly by the *Patisandhi-Citta* (rebirth-linking consciousness).

KARMIC SIGNS: Near death, the mind is flooded with signs:
Kamma: Memories of PAST ACTIONS.
Kamma Nimitta: Symbols of HABITUAL DEEDS (e.g., tools of a trade).
Gati Nimitta: VISIONS OF THE DESTINY to come (e.g., fire for hell, gardens for heaven).

~ The Ultimate Goal ~

NIBBĀNA (*Nirvana*): The "Win Condition" is the CESSATION of the CYCLE.

ACHIEVED: By EXTINGUISHING the "Three Poisons" (GREED, HATRED, DELUSION) and uprooting IGNORANCE.

METHOD: The NOBLE EIGHTFOLD PATH (*Ethics, Meditation, Wisdom*). When the fuel of craving is exhausted, the flame of suffering is blown out.

THE CARTOGRAPHY OF THE GAP

CLASSICAL BUDDHISM focuses on the moment of death and the moment of rebirth. But what happens in the gap between the two? The TIBETAN tradition fills this silence with noise, colour, and terror. It maps the *BARDO*—the intermediate state—as a psychedelic landscape where the mind meets its own projections.

Tibetan Buddhism (Vajrayāna):
The Geography of the In-Between

~ System Profile ~

Type: Cyclical / Psychological / Transitional Flow

Engine: Karma (*Action*) & Lung (*Wind Energy*)

Core Principle: Projection. Death is not an instantaneous switch but a prolonged opportunity for liberation. The reality encountered after death is a projection of the mind's own contents; recognising this leads to freedom.

~ Anatomy of the Traveler ~

Passenger: None (*Anattā*). What continues is the *Sem-gyu* ("Mindstream") — a subtle continuum of luminous awareness, empty of inherent existence but carrying karmic seeds.

Shell: The Physical Body. The elements dissolve at death: Earth into Water, Water into Fire, Fire into Air, Air into Consciousness.

Carrier: The Mental Body. In the later stages of death, the consciousness rides the "karmic winds" (*Lung*) and possesses a subtle body that moves at the speed of thought.

Key Metaphor: *The Cinema Projector.* The deities and landscapes encountered in the afterlife are movies projected by the mind onto the screen of emptiness. "Peaceful and Wrathful Deities" appear, but they are reflections of one's own nature.

ATLAS OF AFTERLIFE COSMOLOGIES

~ Cartography of the Invisible ~

Transition: From DEATH to REBIRTH is mapped as a 49-day journey through specific intervals known as BARDOS ("*In-Betweens*").

Table: 4. The Map of Realms (The Six Bardos)

Bardo Name	State of Consciousness	Description & Experience
Kyene Bardo	**Waking Life**	The ordinary period from birth to the onset of death.
Milam Bardo	**Dream State**	The consciousness experienced during sleep.
Samten Bardo	**Meditation**	The state of deep concentration (*Samadhi*) achieved in life.
Chikhai Bardo	**The Moment of Death**	The dissolution of the elements. The **"Clear Light of Reality"** dawns. **Opportunity:** Instant liberation (*Dharmakāya*) if this light is recognised as one's own nature.
Chönyi Bardo	**Luminosity / Reality**	A psychedelic realm of lights, sounds, and rays. **Peaceful and Wrathful Deities** appear. **Opportunity:** Liberation if one recognizes these terrifying figures as self-projections.
Sidpa Bardo	**Becoming**	The winds of *karma* blow the soul toward rebirth. The spirit possesses a mental body, moves at thought-speed, and seeks a womb based on attraction or aversion to visions of future parents.

~ The Mechanics of Transition ~

DISSOLUTION:	The process begins with the collapse of the physical senses and elements.
SUBTLE ENERGIES:	Wind Energy (*Lung*), drives the consciousness through the intermediate states. If the mind is unstable, these winds blow it like a feather in a storm.
ATTRACTION/ AVERSION:	In the final stage (*Sidpa Bardo*), the consciousness sees visions of copulating couples. Driven by desire (attraction) or anger (aversion), it enters a womb, initiating the next life.

~ The Ultimate Goal ~

BUDDHAHOOD:	The "Win Condition" is full enlightenment, often expressed as the RAINBOW BODY or realising the *Dharmakāya*.
BODHISATTVA:	Alternatively, one may choose to return deliberately. A BODHISATTVA is one who sees the cycle clearly yet vows to remain within it to aid all beings, dissolving self-clinging through service.

The Physics of the Soul

We return from the psychological landscapes of Tibet to the Indian plains to encounter the most rigorous physics of the spirit. In JAINISM, *karma* is not merely a moral law or a mental projection; it is a subtle material substance—a cosmic dust that literally weighs the soul down.

JAINISM: *The Physics of Spiritual Gravity*

~ System Profile ~

Type:	Materialist / Cyclical / Vertical Hierarchy
Engine:	Karmic Matter (*Subtle atomic particles*).
Core Principle:	The soul is naturally buoyant and luminous but is weighed down by the physical accumulation of *karma*. The universe is a closed system of spiritual physics where heavy souls sink and light souls float.

~ Anatomy of the Traveler ~

Passenger:	*Jīva*. The SOUL. It is eternal, formless, conscious, and naturally omniscient and buoyant. It is distinct from the body.
Shell:	The BODY. The physical vessel which is discarded at death.
Carrier:	KARMIC DUST. Subtle atomic matter that adheres to the soul due to passion and activity, creating spiritual "weight" or specific gravity that determines the soul's vertical position in the cosmos.

~ Cartography of the Invisible ~

The JAIN universe is finite and shaped like a colossal standing man, known as the *Loka-Purusha* (The Cosmic Man). The soul's location within this giant body is determined strictly by its karmic weight.

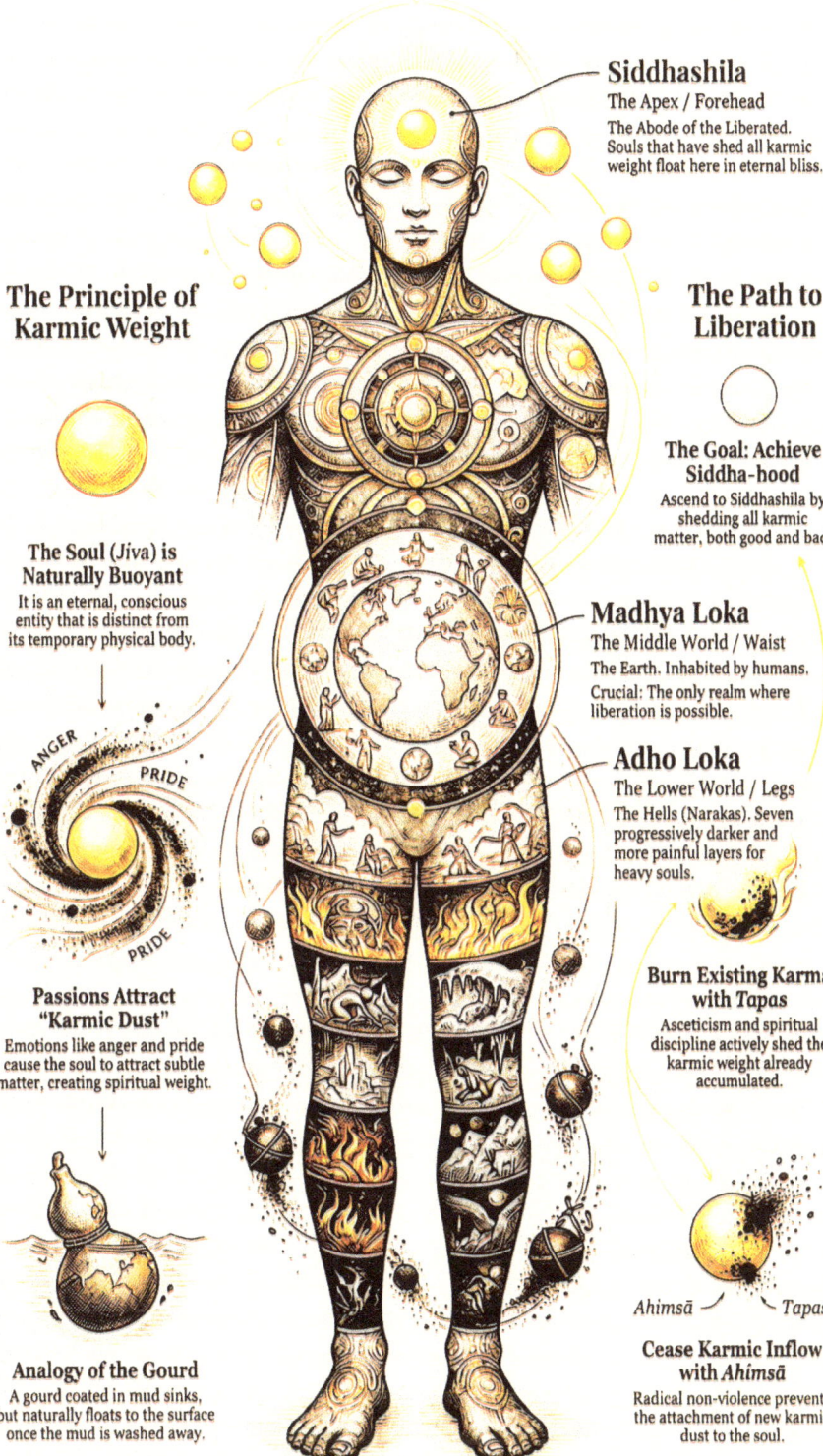

Table 5. The Map of Jain Realms

Realm Group	Location in Cosmic Man	Description & Inhabitants
Siddhaśilā (The Crescent Apex)	The Forehead / Top Edge	The **Abode of the Liberated.** A crescent-shaped realm at the very roof of the cosmos. Souls that have shed *all* weight float here to exist in eternal isolation, omniscience, and bliss.
Urdhva Loka (Upper World)	The Torso and Head	The Heavens. Inhabited by the **Vaimanika Devas** (gods in flying palaces). These are realms of pleasure, but still within the cycle.
Madhya Loka (Middle World)	The Waist	The Earth (*Jambudvipa*). Inhabited by humans and animals. **Crucial:** This is the only realm where liberation (shedding *karma*) is possible.
Adho Loka (Lower World)	The Legs	The Lower Worlds/Hells (**Narakas**). Seven layers that get progressively darker and more painful (e.g., *Ratna prabha* or Jewel-hue; *Tamah prabha* or Darkness-hue).

~ The Mechanics of Transition ~

Vibration + Adhesion: The mechanism is MECHANICAL rather than judicial. Passions such as ANGER, PRIDE, DECEIT, and GREED cause the soul (*jiva*) to vibrate. This vibration makes the soul "moist" or sticky, attracting KARMIC DUST which adheres to it.

Spiritual Gravity: This accumulated DUST creates WEIGHT. Heavy souls sink toward the *Adho Loka* (Hells); lighter souls rise toward the *Urdhva Loka* (Heavens).

THE CYCLE:	"The soul is eternal. It is born again and again, experiencing the fruits of its own actions" (*Tattvārtha Sūtra* 2.10).
KEY ANALOGY:	A gourd coated in mud sinks in water; once the mud (*karma*) is washed away, the gourd naturally floats to the surface.

~ THE ULTIMATE GOAL ~

SIDDHA-HOOD:	The "Win Condition" is to ascend to the SIDDHAŚILĀ.
	This is achieved by shedding *all* karmic matter—both good and bad—thereby restoring the soul's natural buoyancy.
METHOD:	The method is *AHIMSĀ* (radical non-violence) to prevent new dust from attaching, and TAPAS (asceticism) to burn off existing dust.

Type B: The Linear-Ascension Models

Core Principle:

Rectification and *Ascent*. The universe is a ladder or a **refinery**. The soul originates from a Divine Source, descends into matter, and must climb back up through specific spheres of purification to regain its original unity.

We now move West, where the Wheel is replaced by the Ladder. In these traditions, the soul is not trapped in an endless loop of biological rebirths but is on a singular trajectory. It begins with a descent from the Divine and ends with a return to it. The geography here is defined by judgment, purgation, and the restoration of a lost perfection.

Atlas Of Afterlife Cosmologies

ANCIENT EGYPT: *The Weighing of the Heart*

~ SYSTEM PROFILE ~

TYPE:	LINEAR / JUDGMENT-BASED
ENGINE:	MA'AT (COSMIC TRUTH/JUSTICE) & RITUAL PRESERVATION
CORE PRINCIPLE:	PRESERVATION AND RECTIFICATION. The afterlife is a perilous journey requiring both moral purity and ritual knowledge to avoid the "Second Death" (non-existence) and achieve transfiguration.

~ ANATOMY OF THE TRAVELER ~

PASSENGER:	*Ba*. The PERSONALITY or SOUL. Depicted as a bird with a human head, it retains the capability to fly between the tomb and the underworld.
SHELL:	The PHYSICAL BODY. Though not explicitly named in the provided text, it is the anchor for the *Ka* and the subject of "Ritual Preservation" (mummification) to ensure survival.
CARRIER:	*Ka* (THE VITAL SPARK). The life-force that requires sustenance (food/offerings) to survive in the tomb; its union with the *Ba* creates the transfigured spirit, the *Akh*.

~ CARTOGRAPHY OF THE INVISIBLE ~

The Egyptian cosmos maps the afterlife as THE *DUAT*, a perilous underworld landscape of fire, darkness, and gateways guarded by demons. The soul must navigate this terrain using passwords and spells learned from *The Book of the Dead*.

ATLAS OF AFTERLIFE COSMOLOGIES

Table 6. The Map of Egyptian Realms

Realm Name	Description	Inhabitants/Condition
The Duat	**The Underworld.** A dangerous transitional zone filled with hazards that test the soul's knowledge and preparation.	**Demons & Gatekeepers.** Entities that require specific passwords to bypass.
The Hall of Two Truths	**The Judicial Chamber.** The location of the ultimate moral test before 42 judges.	**Osiris, The 42 Judges, & Ammit.** The place of judgment where the soul's innocence is weighed.
Aaru	**The Field of Reeds.** An idealised version of Egypt—a lush, fertile delta where the dead live in peace.	**The Blessed Dead (Akhs) & Gods.** Inhabitants farm and feast eternally in a state of perfection.

~ The Mechanics of Transition ~

NAVIGATION:	The soul traverses the *Duat* using MAGICAL KNOWLEDGE (spells/passwords) to bypass demonic guardians.
THE NEGATIVE CONFESSION:	Upon reaching the HALL OF TWO TRUTHS, the soul stands before 42 JUDGES and declares its INNOCENCE of specific sins (e.g., "I have not stolen," "I have not made anyone cry").
THE WEIGHING OF THE HEART:	The HEART (*Ib*) is placed on a scale against the *Feather of Ma'at* (Truth).
FAILURE:	If the heart is heavy with sin, it is devoured by *AMMIT* (the Devourer), resulting in the "Second Death"—total non-existence.

SUCCESS: If the HEART BALANCES, the soul is declared "True of Voice".

~ The Ultimate Goal ~

TRANSFIGURATION: The "Win Condition" is to become an *Akh* (a TRANSFIGURED SPIRIT) through the union of *Ba* and *Ka*, allowing the entity to dwell among the stars or gods.

PARADISE: Residence in AARU, the FIELD OF REEDS, enjoying an eternal, agrarian life of abundance.

The Rational Cycle

Across the Mediterranean, the Greeks and Romans adopted the EGYPTIAN CONCERN FOR JUDGMENT but stripped away the mummification and rituals. For the philosophers, the afterlife became a place of rational sorting. Here, the soul is not weighed against a feather, but tested by its own wisdom and choices.

THE GRECO-ROMAN MODEL:
The Pedagogical Cycle

~ System Profile ~

Type:	Rational / Choice-Based / Cyclical
Engine:	*Ananke* (Necessity) & Rational Choice
Core Principle:	Education and Refinement. The afterlife is a rational interval of judgment and choice between earthly tenures, where the soul is sculpted back to beauty through virtue and purification.

~ Anatomy of the Traveler ~

Passenger:	*Psyche* (Soul). Immortal, rational, and pre-existent. Often depicted as a *charioteer driving two horses* (Reason and Appetite).
Shell:	*Soma* (Body). The perishable vessel from which the philosopher seeks liberation.
Carrier:	The Daemon. A guiding spirit or genius attached to the soul for a specific lifetime to ensure it fulfils its destiny.

~ Cartography of the Invisible ~

The geography of the afterlife is a moral landscape of judgment, reward, and punishment, governed by cosmic machinery.

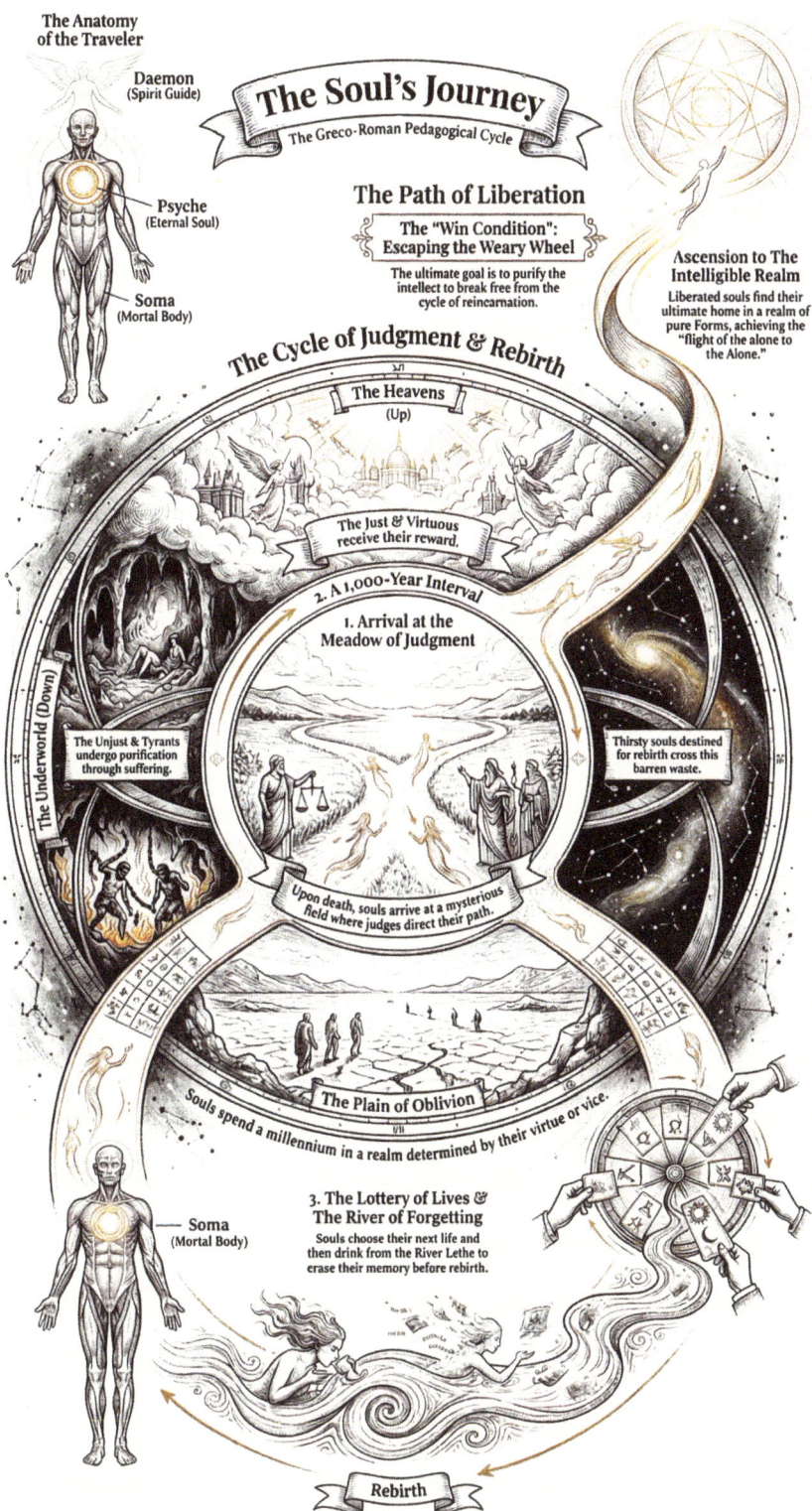

Table 7. The Map of Greco-Roman Realms

Realm Name	Description	Inhabitants/Condition
The Meadow of Judgment	A mysterious field with two openings in the earth and two in the sky. The arrival point for the dead.	**Judges** who direct souls Up (Right) or Down (Left).
The Heavens (Right/Up)	A realm of bliss and order. Souls reside here for 1,000 years as a reward for a just life.	The Just / Virtuous. Beware: Life here can lead to complacency in the next choice.
The Underworld (Left/Down)	A realm of punishment beneath the earth. Souls suffer a tenfold repayment for earthly sins (1,000 years).	The Unjust. Tyrants and criminals undergo purification through suffering.
The Plain of Oblivion	A barren, burning waste that souls must cross before rebirth.	Thirsty souls marching toward the River Lethe.
The Intelligible Realm	(Neoplatonic). The realm of pure Forms and the One.	The ultimate home of the rational soul, reached through the "flight of the alone to the Alone."

~ The Mechanics of Transition ~

Spindle of Necessity: After the 1,000-YEAR INTERVAL, souls gather to view the cosmic machine (*Ananke*) which turns the celestial spheres and produces the HARMONY OF THE SPHERES.

Lottery of Lives: Unlike automatic Eastern *karma*, PLATO emphasises CHOICE. Souls draw lots to determine the order of choosing. PATTERNS OF LIVES (tyrants, animals, citizens) are spread out on the ground. The soul must CHOOSE its next life using the wisdom it gained (or failed to gain).

	Fatal Flaw: A virtuous soul without philosophy may foolishly choose a tyrant's life out of greed, unaware of the suffering attached to it.
THE RIVER LETHE:	The RIVER OF UNMINDFULNESS. Before being shot back into a new birth like a falling star, all souls must DRINK from it to ERASE THEIR MEMORY. The wise drink only enough to survive; the foolish drink heavily and forget everything.

~ THE ULTIMATE GOAL ~

RETURN TO THE ONE:	The "Win Condition" is to escape the "weary wheel" of rebirth.
ACHIEVED	By PURIFYING THE INTELLECT and cutting away the superfluous, like a sculptor revealing a statue.
GOAL:	The VISIO BEATIFICA (Beatific Vision)—contemplating the eternal Forms or the Good.

THE SYNTHESIS OF THE WEST

The fragmented maps of antiquity—the Greek spheres, the Roman underworlds, and the Egyptian moral tests—were eventually gathered and synthesised into a definitive moral architecture by the Christian imagination. Here, the afterlife becomes a singular, linear drama of redemption, where the ultimate goal is not just the liberation of the soul, but the resurrection of the body.

CHRISTIANITY (DANTE'S MODEL):
The Christian Moral Geography

~ SYSTEM PROFILE ~

TYPE: LINEAR / PURGATORIAL / ASCENSION

ENGINE: CONTRAPASSO (*Divine Justice*) & LOVE

CORE PRINCIPLE: RECTIFICATION AND ASCENSION. The universe is a REFINING FIRE and a LADDER. The soul, CREATED BY GOD, must climb back through specific spheres of purification to regain its ORIGINAL UNITY AND GLORIFIED FORM.

~ ANATOMY OF THE TRAVELER ~

PASSENGER: THE SOUL (*Anima*). UNIQUE, created at CONCEPTION (orthodoxy), RATIONAL, and IMMORTAL. It is not pre-existent (in Dante's view) but is the "breath" of GOD.

SHELL: THE BODY. Initially decays, but the ultimate goal is its restoration.

CARRIER: THE RESURRECTED BODY. Unlike dualistic models that discard the body, the ultimate goal here is to regain it in a glorified, incorruptible state to inhabit the New Creation.

~ CARTOGRAPHY OF THE INVISIBLE ~

Dante Alighieri synthesised classical geography and Christian theology into a precise, three-part structural map of the afterlife.

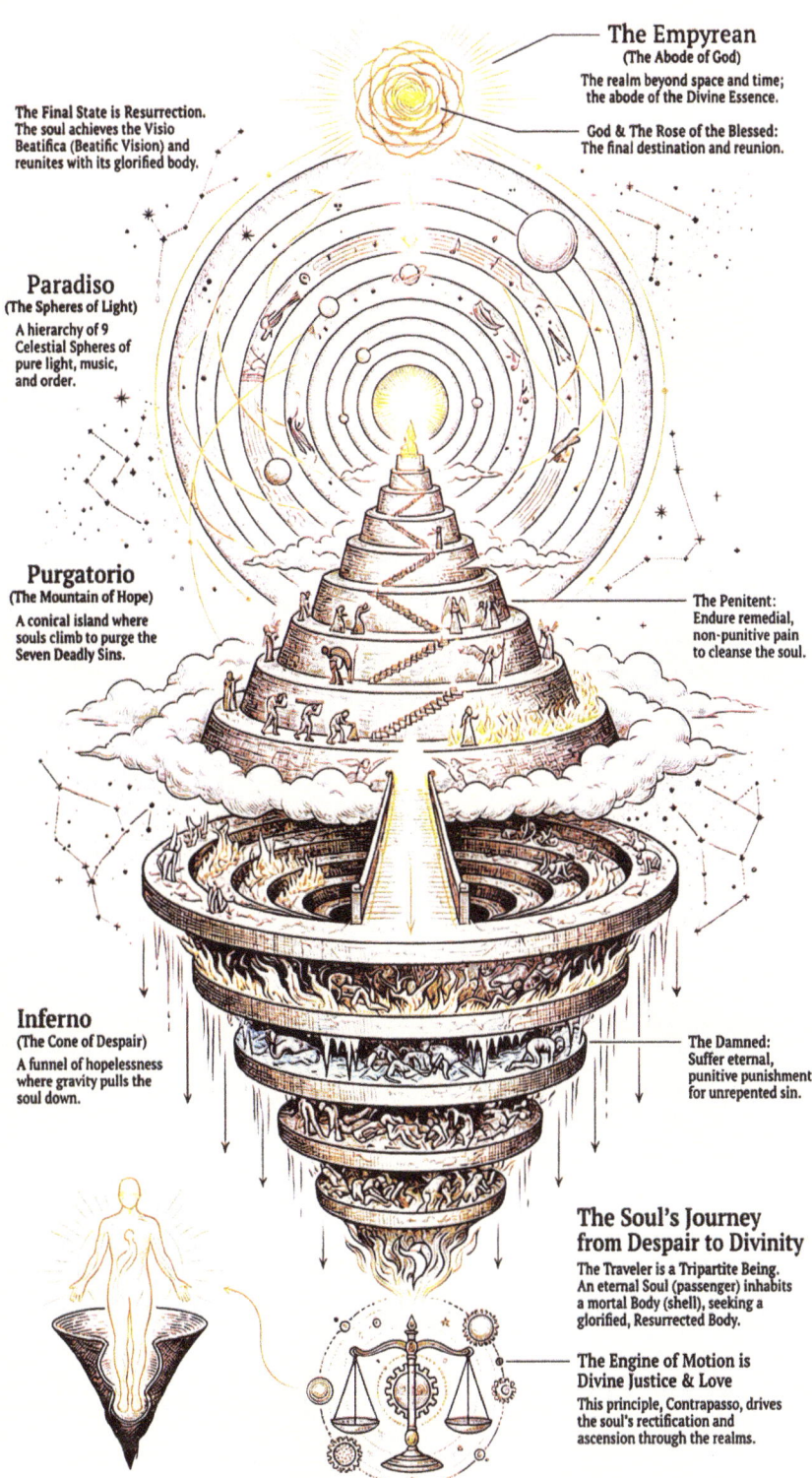

Table 8. The Map of Dante's Realms

Realm Name	Description	Inhabitants/Condition
Inferno (The Cone of Despair)	A FUNNEL descending to the center of the earth. A realm of hopeless stasis and gravity where sin pulls the soul down.	**The Damned.** Those who died unrepentant. Punishment is *Contrapasso*—the sin itself acted out eternally (e.g., the lustful blown by winds).
Purgatorio (The Mountain of Hope)	A conical ISLAND-MOUNTAIN in the southern hemisphere (antipodes of Jerusalem). The only realm where change and time exist.	**The Penitent.** Souls climbing the mountain to purge the Seven Deadly Sins. The pain here is remedial, not punitive.
Paradiso (The Spheres of Light)	A hierarchy of 9 CELESTIAL SPHERES orbiting the earth (Moon to Primum Mobile). A realm of pure light, music, and order.	**The Blessed & Angels.** Arranged according to their capacity to receive Divine Light.
The Empyrean	The realm BEYOND SPACE AND TIME, outside the physical universe.	**God & The Rose of the Blessed.** The abode of the Divine Essence.

~ The Mechanics of Transition ~

GRAVITY VS. GRACE: In *Inferno*, the PHYSICS is SPIRITUAL GRAVITY—the heavier the sin, the deeper the soul sinks toward the centre of the earth (*Cocytus*).

THE CLIMB: In *Purgatorio*, the mechanism is effort. Souls must physically climb the mountain. As a vice is purged (e.g., pride), the letter "P" (*Peccatum*) is erased from their forehead, making the soul lighter and the climb easier.

TRANSHUMANISATION: In *Paradiso*, the soul does not move by feet but by desire. As it aligns its will with GOD ("The Love that moves the sun and the other stars"), it NATURALLY ASCENDS through the spheres.

~ The Ultimate Goal ~

VISIO BEATIFICA: The "Win Condition" is the BEATIFIC VISION—seeing GOD FACE-TO-FACE in the Empyrean.

RESURRECTION: The final state is not disembodied bliss, but the reunion of the purified soul with its glorified body at the end of time.

The Wheel within the Line

While the Church looked upward to resurrection, the mystics of Judaism looked inward and found a wheel turning within the linear timeline. In the Kabbalah, the linear path of "creation to redemption" is complicated by the need for repair (*Tikkun*), allowing the soul to roll back into the world to finish what was left undone.

KABBALAH (JUDAISM): *The Rolling of Souls*

~ System Profile ~

Type:	Esoteric / Repair-Based / Cyclical-Linear Hybrid
Engine:	*Tikkun* (Rectification) & *Gilgul* (Rolling)
Core Principle:	Repair of the World. Souls are divine sparks scattered in broken vessels. They return not for punishment, but to complete specific spiritual missions or fulfil neglected commandments (*mitzvot*), thereby rectifying the cosmos.

~ Anatomy of the Traveler ~

The soul is not a monolith but a composite structure of five levels, originating from the Divine Light:

Passenger:	*Neshamah*: The intellectual/divine soul that connects directly to God.
	Chaya: The living essence (*transcendent*).
	Yechidah: The singularity (*absolute unity with God*).
Shell:	*Guf* (The Body). The physical vessel that returns to dust.
Carrier:	*Nefesh*: The biological/animal soul (*connected to the blood*) that stays near the grave.
	Ruach: The emotional spirit/seat of character that connects the lower and higher souls.

~ Cartography of the Invisible ~

The afterlife geography is focused on purification and eventual bliss, structured around the concept of returning to the Garden.

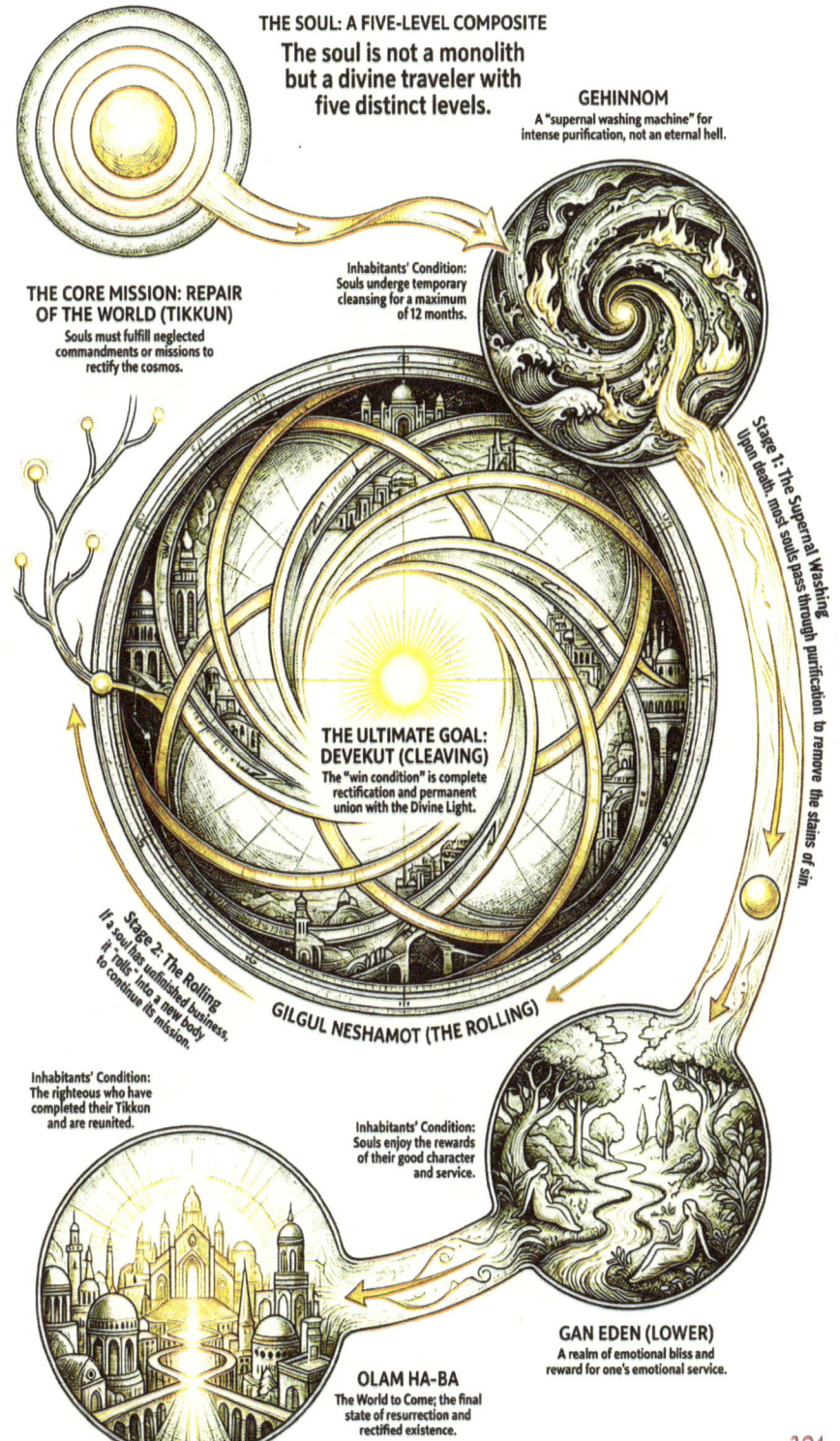

Table 9. The Map of Kabbalistic Realms

Realm Name	Description	Inhabitants/Condition
Gehinnom	Not an eternal hell, but a "supernal washing machine." A place of intense purification where the heat of shame burns away the impurities of the ego.	Souls undergoing temporary cleansing (usually limited to a maximum of 12 months).
Gan Eden (Lower)	The Lower Garden of Eden. A realm of emotional bliss.	Souls enjoying the rewards of their emotional service and character.
Gan Eden (Upper)	The Upper Garden of Eden. A realm of intellectual and spiritual bliss.	Souls enjoying the deep understanding of Torah and divine secrets.
Olam Ha-Ba	The World to Come. The final state of resurrection, clarity, and rectified existence.	The righteous of all nations who have completed their *tikkun*.

~ The Mechanics of Transition ~

Supernal Washing: Upon death, most souls pass through *Gehinnom* for a period of purification (max 12 months) to remove the stains of sin before entering Paradise.

Gilgul Neshamot:	(The Rolling) If a soul has unfinished business, it undergoes *Gilgul*. It "rolls" into a new body to: - Fulfil specific *mitzvot* (commandments) it neglected. - Rectify a relationship or wrong done to another.
Ibbur:	(Impregnation): A specialised mechanism where a righteous soul temporarily "possesses" or attaches itself to a living person to assist them in a task or complete a specific mission, then departs.

~ The Ultimate Goal ~

Devekut	(Cleaving) The "Win Condition" is complete rectification (*Tikkun*) and permanent union with the Divine Light.
Resurrection:	The ultimate horizon is the resurrection of the dead in a perfected world, where body and soul are reunited in holiness.

SUFI ISLAM: *The Alchemy of Fanā' and Baqā'*

~ SYSTEM PROFILE ~

TYPE: EMANATIONIST / ASCENT (*Linear with Cyclical undertones*)

ENGINE: 'ISHQ (*Divine Love*) & PURIFICATION (*Jihād al-Nafs*)

CORE PRINCIPLE: THE RETURN OF THE DROP. The SOUL is a BREATH of the DIVINE SPIRIT VEILED BY EGO. The journey is an ascent through cosmic realms, "dying" to lower states to awaken in higher ones, until the drop returns to the Ocean.

~ ANATOMY OF THE TRAVELER ~

PASSENGER: *Rūḥ* (SPIRIT). A breath of the Divine, inherently pure and longing for its source.

SHELL: *Jism* (BODY). The cage or vessel made of clay (earthly elements).

CARRIER: *Nafs* (SELF/SOUL). The battleground of consciousness. It must evolve from the commanding self (*Nafs al-ammārah*) to the contented self (*Nafs al-muṭma'innah*) to CARRY THE SPIRIT HOME.

~ CARTOGRAPHY OF THE INVISIBLE ~

The Sufi cosmos is a hierarchy of FIVE DIVINE PRESENCES (*Hadarat*), representing levels of proximity to Reality. The soul travels upward through these worlds.

Table 10. The Map of Islamic Realms

Realm Name	Description	Inhabitants/Condition
Alam-i-Nasut	The WORLD OF HUMANITY. The physical, sensory world of bodies and matter.	Humans, animals, minerals. The realm of separation and testing.
Alam-i-Malakut	The WORLD OF SOVEREIGNTY. The angelic or subtle realm; the world of souls and imaginal forms (*Mithal*).	Angels, spirits, and souls in the intermediate state (*Barzakh*).
Alam-i-Jabarut	The WORLD OF POWER. The realm of Archangelic power and Divine Decree.	Archangels and high celestial forces. A realm of immense spiritual energy.
Alam-i-Lahut	The WORLD OF DIVINITY. The realm of the Divine Names and Attributes (*Theophany*).	Manifestations of GOD's qualities (Mercy, Majesty, Light).
Alam-i-Hahut	The World of "HE-NESS." The Essence of GOD.	The Unknowable, Absolute Reality. The Source beyond all definition.

~ The Mechanics of Transition ~

The Cage and the Bird:	DEATH is the breaking of the cage, allowing the bird (soul) to fly.

ATLAS OF AFTERLIFE COSMOLOGIES

DIE BEFORE YOU DIE: The TRANSITION is not just a physical event but a spiritual practice. By ANNIHILATING the EGO (*Fanā*) while alive, the Sufi practices the final ascent.

EVOLUTIONARY ASCENT: While ORTHODOX ISLAM rejects REINCARNATION (*tanasukh*) as a return to earth, SUFI POETRY (e.g., Rumi) describes an ascent of consciousness: "I died as a mineral and became a plant, I died as plant and rose to animal..." This implies a cyclical evolution of form towards the Human, and from Human to Angel.

THE CARAVAN: Life is a caravan journeying from the Source BACK TO THE SOURCE. Death is simply the next stage of travel.

~ The Ultimate Goal ~

FANĀ' & BAQĀ': The "Win Condition" is twofold:

FANĀ': ANNIHILATION of the SELF in GOD (The drop disappearing).

BAQĀ': SUBSISTENCE in GOD (The drop becoming the Ocean).

THE REED FLUTE: The goal is to END the "CRYING" of SEPARATION and RETURN to the reed-bed (the Divine Source).

Type C: The Ancestral Continuum

Core Principle:

PARALLELISM AND RECIPROCITY. THE AFTERLIFE IS NOT "UP" OR "down," but "right here." It is a parallel dimension intimately connected to the living. The dead become Ancestors who require sustenance and provide protection.

Finally, we turn to traditions where the boundary between life and death is permeable. Here, the goal is not to escape the world (as in India) nor to ascend out of it (as in the West), but to maintain the flow of life within it. The dead do not vanish into distant heavens; they move into the invisible neighbourhood, maintaining a watchful eye on their lineage. THE DEAD ARE STILL HERE.

ATLAS OF AFTERLIFE COSMOLOGIES

The Celtic Tradition:
The Ever-Living Ones

The Traveler is a Trinity

- Soul (Passenger)
- Body (Temporary Shell)
- Memory/Song (Vehicle)

Death is a Passageway
Viewed as the midpoint of a long life, death is a transition to a parallel realm, the Sidhe (Hollow Hills), not an end.

The Goal is Ancestral Presence
The soul's aim is to join the "Ever-Living Ones," either through rebirth or by dwelling in the Otherworld.

The Yoruba Tradition:
The Marketplace & The Home

The Traveler Carries Destiny

Ori (Soul · Chooses Destiny)

The soul (Emi) chooses its destiny before birth; the Body is a vessel for the "marketplace" of Earth.

Good Heaven (Orun Rere) — Spiritual Rubbish Heap

Judgment is Based on Character
After life's "business trip," a soul's character (Iwa) determines its destination: Good Heaven (Orun Rere) or a spiritual rubbish heap.

The Goal is Revered Ancestor-hood
The aim is to become a revered ancestral spirit (Egungun), maintaining balance and reincarnating parts of their essence within the family.

The Daoist Tradition:
The Bureaucracy of Hell

The Traveler is a Duality

- Hun (Yang Soul · Ascends)
- Po (Yin Soul · Returns to Earth)

Death is a Bureaucratic Trial
The soul is processed through the ten courts of the Underworld (Diyu), facing judgment and punishment like in an imperial administration.

Tea of Oblivion

The Goal is Karmic Cleansing & Rebirth
After serving its sentence, the soul drinks a tea of oblivion and is returned to the Wheel of Reincarnation for a clean slate.

212

THE CELTIC TRADITION: *The Ever-Living Ones*

~ SYSTEM PROFILE ~

TYPE: ANCESTRAL CONTINUUM / TRANSMIGRATION

ENGINE: LINEAGE, MEMORY & HEROIC VIRTUE

CORE PRINCIPLE: THE MIDPOINT OF A LONG LIFE. DEATH is not a TERMINATION but a "passageway" or a "change of clothes." Existence is an ETERNAL RHYTHM where the soul does not perish but passes from one body to another, sustaining the courage of the living.

~ ANATOMY OF THE TRAVELER ~

PASSENGER: THE SOUL. IMMUTABLE and IMMORTAL. It is a shape-shifter that retains a core of awareness across lives (as described by the poet *Taliesin*: "I have been a drop... a star... a word").

SHELL: THE BODY. A TEMPORARY VESSEL. Because the soul survives, the body is treated with respect but without attachment—warriors bury weapons and goods with it, not as final tributes, but as provisions for a continued journey.

CARRIER: MEMORY & SONG. While the soul TRANSMIGRATES, the *social* identity is carried by the BARDS. To be remembered in song is to remain active in the world of the living.

~ CARTOGRAPHY OF THE INVISIBLE ~

The Celtic cosmos is not vertical (Heaven/Hell) but parallel. The "Otherworld" exists alongside the physical world, hidden behind a thin veil or within the landscape itself.

ATLAS OF AFTERLIFE COSMOLOGIES

ANATOMY OF THE TRAVELER

THE SOUL: THE IMMORTAL PASSENGER
An eternal, shape-shifting part that retains awareness across lifetimes.

THE ULTIMATE GOAL: ANCESTRAL PRESENCE
To join the Ever-Living Ones by returning to the clan or dwelling in the Sídhe.

MEMORY & SONG: THE SOCIAL VEHICLE
Carries social identity so the person is remembered and remains active in the world.

DEATH IS THE "PASSAGEWAY"
Viewed as the midpoint of a long life, not the end.

THE BODY: THE TEMPORARY SHELL
A respected vessel for the soul, but one without ultimate attachment.

THE PARALLEL REALMS OF EXISTENCE

THE EARTHLY WORLD
The realm of battle, harvest, and clan life.
Inhabitants: Humans living out their destiny.

THE VEIL (SAMHAIN)
The temporary boundary between worlds, thinning to allow passage.
Inhabitants: Wandering souls and Ancestors returning.

THE SÍDHE (HOLLOW HILLS)
The Otherworld, a sea of eternal youth where time flows differently.
Inhabitants: The Aes Sidhe (The Ever-Living Ones)

Table 11. The Map of Celtic Realms

Realm Name	Description	Inhabitants/Condition
The Earthly World	The realm of battle, harvest, and clan life.	Humans living out their destiny and demonstrating courage.
The Sídhe (*The Hollow Hills*)	The OTHERWORLD, often located inside ancient burial mounds or across the sea. A realm of eternal youth and beauty where time flows differently.	**The Aes Sídhe** (The Ever-Living Ones) and the *Tuatha Dé Danann* (Divine Ancestors).
The Veil (*Samhain*)	The TEMPORAL BOUNDARY BETWEEN WORLDS. During the festival of *Samhain* (Nov 1), this barrier thins, allowing traffic between the living and the dead.	Wandering souls and Ancestors returning to visit their kin.

~ The Mechanics of Transition ~

Metempsychōsis (*Transmigration*): As reported by Julius Caesar and Lucan, the Druidic teaching is explicit: "Souls do not perish, but after death pass from one body to another."

The Passageway: Death is viewed as the "midpoint of a long life" rather than its end. This belief serves a specific psychological function: the

	elimination of the fear of death, encouraging absolute valour in battle.
RECIPROCITY:	The transition is supported by the living. Grave goods (food, weapons, chariots) are provided because the deceased is merely moving to another location or state of being where these items will still be useful.

~ The Ultimate Goal ~

COURAGE & CONTINUITY:	The "Win Condition" is to face death without fear.
ANCESTRAL PRESENCE:	To join the EVER-LIVING ONES—either by returning to the clan through rebirth or by dwelling in the *Sídhe*—and to be immortalised in the collective memory of the tribe.

YORUBA TRADITION:
The Marketplace and the Home

~ SYSTEM PROFILE ~

TYPE: ANCESTRAL CONTINUUM / REINCARNATION WITHIN LINEAGE

ENGINE: ORI (*Destiny*) & ÌWÀ (*Character*)

CORE PRINCIPLE: PARALLELISM AND RECIPROCITY. LIFE is a TEMPORARY "business trip" to the marketplace (*Aye*), while Heaven (*Orun*) is the true home to which one returns. The two worlds are intimately connected through the flow of life force.

~ ANATOMY OF THE TRAVELER ~

PASSENGER: *Ori* (THE INNER HEAD). The seat of DESTINY and the DIVINE SPARK. Before birth, the soul kneels before *Olodumare* (GOD) to choose its *Ayanmó* (DESTINY); success in life depends on aligning with this choice.

SHELL: THE PHYSICAL BODY. The vessel used for the "business trip" in the MARKETPLACE of Earth.

CARRIER: *Emi* (THE BREATH). The vital force that animates the living being.

~ CARTOGRAPHY OF THE INVISIBLE ~

The Yoruba cosmos is not a vertical ladder but a binary system of "Home" and "Market," interacting constantly. The dead do not simply leave; they transition to the invisible aspect of the community.

ATLAS OF AFTERLIFE COSMOLOGIES

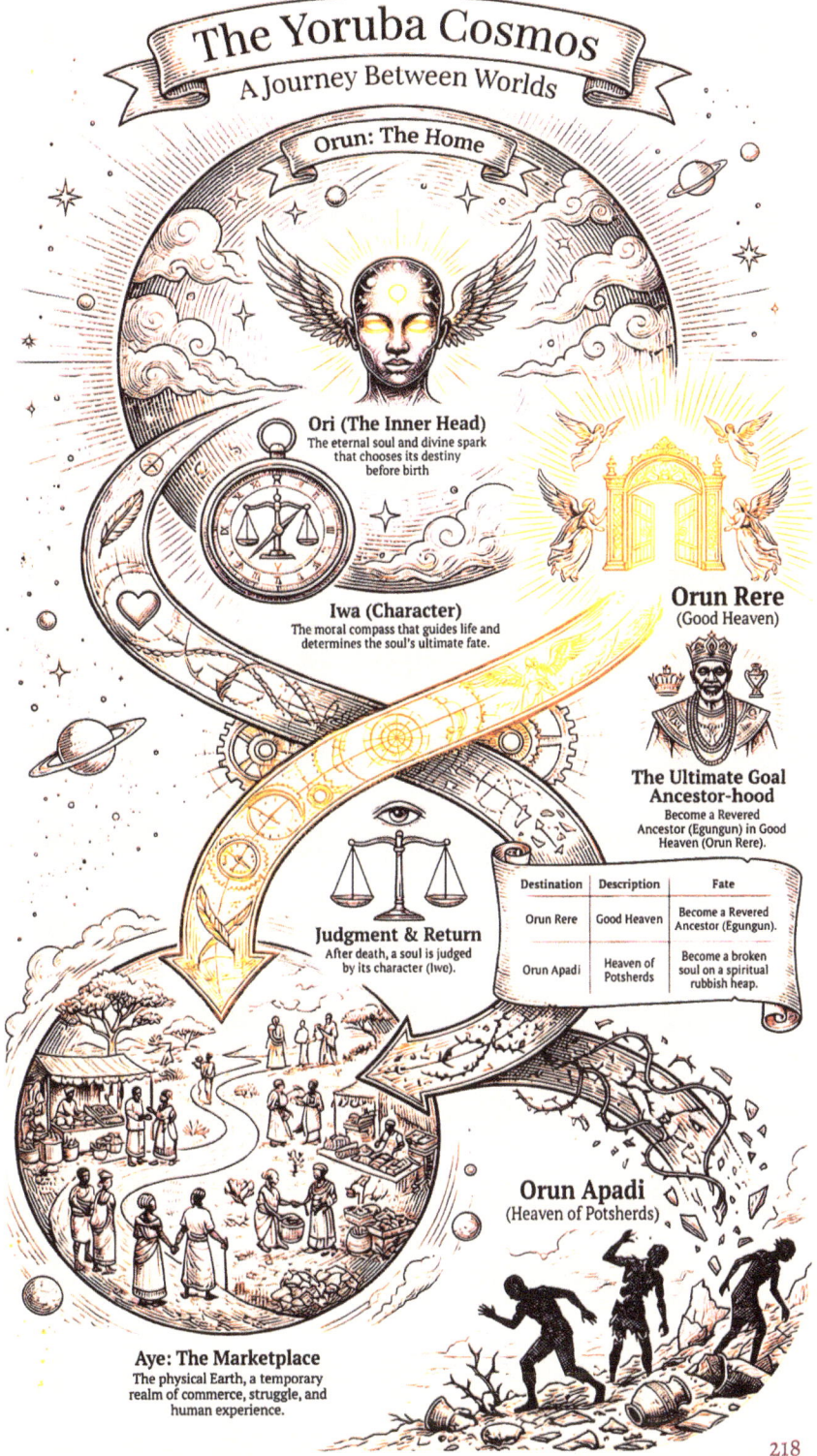

Table 12. The Map of Yorubic Realms

Realm Name	Description	Inhabitants/Condition
Aye (The Earth)	**The Marketplace** (*Loja*). A place of commerce, struggle, and temporary visitation. "The world is a marketplace; heaven is home" (*Aye loja, Òrun nile*).	Living humans and visiting spirits.
Orun (Heaven)	**The Home** (*Nile*). The place of origin, return, and permanent residence.	The Supreme Being (*Olodumare*), Deities (*Orishas*), and Ancestors.
Orun Rere	**Good Heaven.** An ancestral village that mirrors the best of earthly life.	**Egungun** (Revered Ancestral Spirits) who maintain connection with the living.
Orun Apadi	**Heaven of Potsherds.** A spiritual rubbish heap.	The wicked and broken souls, suffering dryness and isolation.

~ The Mechanics of Transition ~

Choosing Destiny: Before the transition to life, the soul CHOOSES its *Ayanmó* (DESTINY) before the Creator.

Judgment: Upon the return home (DEATH), the soul faces judgment based on *Ìwà* (CHARACTER). Good character leads to *Òrun Rere*; wickedness leads to *Òrun Apadi*.

ATÙNWÁ	(*Ancestral Rebirth*): Reincarnation is FAMILIAL and PARTIAL. The ancestor does not vanish from *Òrun* to be born on *Ayé*. Instead, they "shoot forth" a part of their essence into a NEW CHILD WITHIN the SAME FAMILY BLOODLINE.
EVIDENCE:	This mechanism is confirmed when children are identified as RETURNING ELDERS, bearing names like *Babatunde* ("Father returns") or *Yetunde* ("Mother returns").

~ THE ULTIMATE GOAL ~

ANCESTOR-HOOD:	The "Win Condition" is to become a revered ANCESTRAL SPIRIT (*Egungun*)
MAINTENANCE:	The goal is not to escape the world, but to MAINTAIN the COSMIC BALANCE between the MARKETPLACE and the HOME, ensuring the prosperity of the lineage.

THE AKAN TRADITION:
The Return of the Sunsum

~ SYSTEM PROFILE ~

TYPE: ANCESTRAL CONTINUUM / DUAL-SOUL / DUTY-BASED

ENGINE: NKRABEA (*Destiny*) & ANCESTRAL DUTY

CORE PRINCIPLE: PARTIAL REINCARNATION. The human being is a compound entity; upon death, the divine spark returns to the Creator (*Nyame*), while the personality remains to sustain the lineage, ensuring that "the tree remembers" what the axe forgets.

~ ANATOMY OF THE TRAVELER ~

The Akan person is a convergence of three distinct spiritual substances:

PASSENGER: *Okra.* The SOUL or SPARK of GOD (*Nyame*). It carries the individual's *Nkrabea* (DESTINY) and returns to the Creator upon death.

Ntoro (SPIRIT/CHARACTER). While the *Mogya* (blood) comes from the mother, the *Ntoro* is transmitted from the father. It provides the spiritual character, personality traits, and protection of the father's ancestral deity.

SHELL: *Mogya* (BLOOD). The biological link that belongs to the matrilineal clan (*Abusua*). It ties the individual to the earth and the family.

CARRIER: *Sunsum.* The PERSONALITY, EGO, or SPIRIT. It is the agency of character that survives death, travels to the world of ancestors, and MAY BE REBORN TO FULFIL DESTINY.

ATLAS OF AFTERLIFE COSMOLOGIES

The Akan tradition conceptualizes the human being as a composite of spiritual substances. Upon death, a person's spirit embarks on a journey to the ancestral realm, a process that is crucial for maintaining the continuity and memory of the family lineage.

ANATOMY OF THE TRAVELER

The Okra: The Eternal Passenger
The divine soul or spark of God that carries an individual's destiny (*Nkrabea*).

The Mogya: The Mortal Shell
The biological blood link that ties a person to their matrilineal clan (*Abusua*).

The Sunsum: The Vehicle
The ego or personality that survives death, travels, and can be reborn into the lineage.

THE JOURNEY AFTER DEATH

Asamando: The World of Spirits/Ancestors; a mirror of the living world.

Inhabitants: *Nsamanfo* (Ancestors).

The Destination & Rebirth: The goal is to become an Ancestor, allowing the *Sunsum* to be reborn within the lineage.

The River: Boundary between the living and the dead.

Step 2: The Toll – Paid to Amokye, the ferryman, to pass.

Step 1: The Crossing – The deceased must cross a river to reach *Asamando*, the world of spirits.

The Wilderness: A liminal space for those who fail the crossing.

Saman (Wandering Ghosts): Spirits without proper rites.

KEY REALMS IN THE AKAN SPIRITUAL LANDSCAPE

Asamando
The World of Spirits/Ancestors; a mirror of the living world.

Inhabitants:
Nsamanfo (Ancestors).
The *Sunsum* resides here.

The River
The boundary between the living and the dead.

Inhabitants:
Amokye (The Ferryman) guards the crossing.

The Wilderness
A liminal space for those who fail the crossing.

Inhabitants:
Saman (Wandering Ghosts). Spirits without proper rites.

~ Cartography of the Invisible ~

The afterlife is not a distant heaven but a PARALLEL GEOGRAPHY known as *Asamando*. It exists tangibly, often located across a river, mirroring the structure of the living community.

Table 13. The Map of Akan Realms

Realm Name	Description	Inhabitants/ Condition
Asamando	The WORLD OF SPIRITS/ ANCESTORS. A geographic mirror of the living world, organised by clan and status, but devoid of disease or sorrow.	**Nsamanfo** (Ancestors). The *Sunsum* resides here, maintaining influence over the living.
The River	The BOUNDARY between the LIVING and the DEAD.	**Amokye** (The Ferryman/Woman) who guards the crossing.
The Wilderness	The LIMINAL SPACE for those who fail the crossing.	**Saman** (Wandering Ghosts). Spirits who were not buried with rites or could not pay the toll.

~ The Mechanics of Transition ~

THE CROSSING:	Upon death, the deceased must cross a river to reach *Asamando*.
THE TOLL:	The FERRYMAN, *Amokye*, demands a FEE for PASSAGE. This necessitates the funeral custom of burying the body with gold dust or beads.

RITUAL NECESSITY: If the proper rites are NOT PERFORMED or the TOLL IS NOT PAID, the spirit is DENIED ENTRY and becomes a *Saman* (wandering ghost) that HAUNTS the living.

REBIRTH (PARTIAL):   While the *Okra* returns to GOD, the *Sunsum* can be reborn within the lineage to complete its *Nkrabea* (DESTINY). This is not the return of the *same* individual, but the return of their characteristics and mission.

~ The Ultimate Goal ~

MAINTENANCE: Of Lineage: The "Win Condition" is to become a RESPECTED ANCESTOR in *Asamando*.

TREE METAPHOR: "The axe forgets, but the tree remembers." The individual (the axe) may PERISH, but the lineage (the tree) RETAINS the MEMORY and VITALITY OF THE DEAD, growing again through the return of the *Sunsum*.

From the Village to the Bureaucracy

The reverence for ancestors connects the indigenous traditions of West Africa with the folk religions of East Asia. However, as we move to China, the organic relationship between the living and the dead is overlaid with the structure of imperial administration. The afterlife becomes not just a village, but a government.

Daoism & Chinese Folk Religion:
The Bureaucracy of Hell

~ System Profile ~

Type: Administrative / Purgatorial

Engine: Balance (*Yin/Yang*) & Imperial Bureaucracy

Core Principle: As Above, So Below. The AFTERLIFE is a MIRROR of the IMPERIAL GOVERNMENT ON EARTH, complete with magistrates, paperwork, and corruption. It is a vast administration designed to SETTLE KARMIC DEBTS through JUDGMENT and PUNISHMENT before processing the soul for rebirth.

~ Anatomy of the Traveler ~

The self is a dualistic entity that separates at death:

Passenger: *Hun* (*The Yang Soul*). Light and ethereal. It ascends to heaven or resides in the ancestral tablet to receive offerings.

Shell: *Po* (*The Yin Soul*). Heavy and corporeal. It stays with the corpse, returning to the earth.

Carrier: The Soul under Judgment. While the *Hun* and *Po* separate, the consciousness travels through the underworld bureaucracy to answer for its deeds.

~ Cartography of the Invisible ~

The geography of the dead is mapped as *Diyu* (*The Earth Prison*), a terrifyingly organised purgatory governed by strict laws and overseen by divine administrators.

ATLAS OF AFTERLIFE COSMOLOGIES

Table 14. The Map of Daoist Realms

Realm Name	Description	Inhabitants/Condition
Diyu	The **Earth Prison/Underworld**. A mirror of earthly bureaucracy involving tribunals and torture chambers.	The **Yama Kings** (Judges), Magistrates, Demons, and Souls awaiting trial.
The First Court	The intake centre and place of initial judgment. Contains the **Mirror of Retribution**, which forces the soul to view its past deeds.	Souls facing the evidence of their life.
The Intermediate Courts	Specific penitentiaries designed for specific sins. Landscapes include the **Hill of Knives** and the **Cauldron of Oil**.	Souls undergoing specific, temporary tortures to burn off heavy *karma*.
The Tenth Court	The exit terminal. The location of the **Wheel of Reincarnation**.	Souls who have served their sentences and are prepared for rebirth.

~ The Mechanics of Transition ~

BUREAUCRATIC PROCESS:	Death initiates a LEGAL PROCESS. The soul moves from court to court, judged by the *YAMA KINGS* based on the records of their life.
RETRIBUTION:	Punishment is SPECIFIC and CORRECTIVE (e.g., specific tortures for specific sins).
OBLIVION:	Before stepping onto the *WHEEL OF REINCARNATION* in the TENTH COURT, the SOUL is given *Meng Po's Soup*. This magical draught induces TOTAL AMNESTY and OBLIVION, erasing all memory of the previous life and the time spent in hell to ensure a clean slate for the next birth.

~ The Ultimate Goal ~

REBIRTH:	The primary outcome is to return to the world of the living via the *WHEEL OF REINCARNATION*.
ANCESTRAL STATUS:	For the *Hun* soul, the goal is to be installed in the ANCESTRAL TABLET, maintaining a connection of protection and sustenance with living descendants.

SHINTO: *The Way of the Kami*

~ SYSTEM PROFILE ~

TYPE: PURE VS. POLLUTED / ANCESTRAL CONTINUUM

ENGINE: *KEGARE* (*Pollution*) & *HARAE* (*Purification*)

CORE PRINCIPLE: RESTORATION OF PURITY. The world is ALIVE with divine presence (*Kami*). Death is not an end but a FORM OF IMPURITY (*kegare*) that must be cleansed; the dead do not "leave" but become ancestral guardians in a reciprocal ecosystem with the living.

~ ANATOMY OF THE TRAVELER ~

PASSENGER: *Tamashii / Mitama*. The SPIRIT or SOUL. Upon death, it can become a *Kami* if purified and venerated.

SHELL: THE CORPSE. A source of POLLUTION (*kegare*) that requires ritual separation from the community to avoid spiritual contagion.

CARRIER: ANCESTRAL SPIRIT. The purified state of the soul that allows it to reside within the household altar (*kamidana*) and interact with the living.

~ CARTOGRAPHY OF THE INVISIBLE ~

Shinto cosmology does not focus on a vertical heaven/hell dichotomy but on the proximity of spirits and the state of purity. The barrier between the living and the dead is thin and permeable.

ATLAS OF AFTERLIFE COSMOLOGIES

Takamagahara
The High Plain of Heaven; a realm of order.
Inhabitants: The celestial gods
(Kami) and Amaterasu.

4. The Ultimate Goal
The spirit merges with the collective lineage to become a divine Kami, or god.

Ashihara-no-Nakatsukuni
The Central Land of Reed Plains; the physical world.
Inhabitants: Humans and Nature Spirits.

3. Proximity & Reciprocity
The purified spirit is installed in the household altar (kamidana), co-existing with the living.

Yomi-no-kuni
The World of Darkness; a gloomy land of decay.
Inhabitants: The Dead who have not been purified.

2. Purification (*Harae*)
Ritual cleansing transforms the spirit into a benevolent, venerated ancestor.

1. Pollution (*Kegare*)
Death creates a state of spiritual heaviness that separates the dead from the living.

Tokoyo-no-kuni
The Eternal Land; a 'far-off land' of renewal.
Inhabitants: Spirits of the sea and eternal life.

Table 15. The Map of Shinto Realms

Realm Name	Description	Inhabitants/Condition
Takamagahara	The High Plain of Heaven. The dwelling place of the heavenly *Kami*.	**Amaterasu** and the celestial gods. A realm of order and light.
Ashihara-no-Nakatsukuni	The Central Land of Reed Plains. The physical world (Japan).	**Humans & Nature Spirits.** The realm where life and ritual take place.
Yomi-no-Kuni	The World of Darkness. A gloomy, subterranean land of decay and impurity, similar to the Greek Hades.	**The Dead** who have not been purified. A place of stagnation, not punishment.
Tokoyo-no-Kuni	The Eternal Land. A concept of a "far-off land" across the sea, associated with immortality and renewal.	Spirits associated with the sea and eternal life.

~ The Mechanics of Transition ~

POLLUTION:	(*Kegare*) Death creates a state of HEAVINESS and STAGNATION. The initial transition involves SEPARATING the dead from the living to PREVENT this pollution from spreading.
PURIFICATION:	(*Harae*) Through RITUALS, the spirit is cleansed of *kegare*. This transforms the potentially dangerous ghost into a benevolent ancestor.
PROXIMITY:	The dead do not journey to a distant judgment. They remain "right here." They are installed as GUESTS in the household altar (*Kamidana*), receiving daily offerings of water, rice, and salt.
RECIPROCITY:	The relationship is MUTUAL. The living sustain the ancestors through veneration; the ancestors protect the living through their spiritual influence.

~ The Ultimate Goal ~

KAMI NATURE:	The "Win Condition" is to become a *Kami* (SPIRIT/GOD).
ANCESTRAL STATUS:	To LOSE INDIVIDUAL DISTINCTION and merge with the collective ancestral spirit of the family or clan, maintaining the harmony of the lineage from the invisible side.

You, Again

REVIEWING THE MAP

WE HAVE TRAVERSED THE HIGH-RISES OF HINDU *KARMA*, navigated the psychological *bardos* of Tibet, stood before the scales of Egyptian *Ma'at*, and climbed the purgatorial mountains of the West. We have seen souls recycled like water, refined like gold, and welcomed home like traveling elders.

Though the terrain varies, the compass points remain the same: human life is not an accident, death is not a termination, and our actions carry a weight that pulls us toward our future.

TABLE 16. REVIEWING THE SYSTEMS AND MODELS

System	The Body Is...	The Soul Is...	Death Is...	The Goal Is...
CYCLICAL (*India*)	A GARMENT; a VEHICLE.	A TRAVELER; a PASSENGER.	Taking off clothes.	Exit: Getting off the wheel (*Mokṣa*).
ASCENSION (*West*)	A VESSEL; a STATUE.	A SPARK; a BREATH.	Breaking the shell.	Return: Union with the Source (*Devekut*).
ANCESTRAL (*Indigenous*)	A MASK; a HOUSE.	An ELDER; a GUARDIAN.	Returning home (Nile).	Maintain: Sustaining the lineage (Ancestorhood)

Table 17. Synthesis – The Comparative Atlas

Dimension	CYCLICAL (*India*)	LINEAR-ASCENSION (*West*)	ANCESTRAL (*Indigenous*)
The ENGINE	**KARMA:** Automated moral causality.	**JUDGMENT:** Rational choice or Divine decree.	**RECIPROCITY:** Duty between living and dead.
The GEOGRAPHY	**VERTICAL HIGH-RISE:** 14 *Lokas* or 6 Realms.	**LADDER/REFINERY:** Spheres, Terraces, or Emanations.	**PARALLEL WORLD:** The Village or Marketplace next door.
The TRANSITION	**INSTANT/BARDO:** Immediate transfer or projection.	**PURGATORIAL:** A long duration of cleansing (e.g., 1,000 years).	**THE CROSSING:** A river or boundary requiring a toll/guide.
The GOAL	**EXIT:** Getting *off* the wheel (*Mokṣa*).	**UNION:** Returning to the Source/GOD.	**MAINTENANCE:** Sustaining the lineage (Ancestor-hood).

This structural analysis reveals that the human map of death is defined by a tension between CIRCULARITY (the return to earth) and LINEARITY (the ascent to the divine). The East (India) and the Indigenous traditions emphasise the Cycle—either as a trap to be escaped (Buddhism) or a garden to be tended (Yoruba). The West (Platonism/Monotheism) emphasises the Ascent—a ladder climbing out of the pit of matter toward the light of the One. Yet, in their esoteric hearts, they often meet: the Kabbalist's *Gilgul* looks like *Karma*; the Buddhist's *Bardo* looks like Purgatory; and the Yoruba's *Atúnwá* looks like the eternal return of the spring.

WORKS CITED

HINDUISM

THE BHAGAVAD GITA: Often referred to as the "Gita," this 700-verse scripture is part of the epic Mahabharata. It takes the form of a dialogue between Prince Arjuna and Lord Krishna on a battlefield, addressing duty (*dharma*) and the nature of reality. The text famously describes the soul as eternal and indestructible, casting off worn bodies like old clothes to take on new ones.

THE UPANISHADS: A collection of ancient philosophical texts that explore the nature of reality (*Brahman*) and the self (*Ātman*). They move beyond ritual sacrifice to inner contemplation, introducing key concepts like *karma* (action and consequence) and *saṃsāra* (the cycle of rebirth).

THE VISHNU PURANA: One of the eighteen *Mahapuranas*, this text offers a detailed cosmology of the universe. It maps out the fourteen planetary systems (*lokas*), describing the seven upper worlds of light and the seven lower subterranean heavens, providing a structured geography for the soul's migration.

BUDDHISM

THE PALI CANON (TIPITAKA): The standard collection of scriptures in the *Theravada* Buddhist tradition. It contains the Buddha's teachings on the Four Noble Truths, the Eightfold Path, and the doctrine of *anattā* (no-self), explaining how rebirth occurs as a causal continuum rather than the migration of a permanent soul.

THE MILINDA PANHA (Questions of King Milinda): A famous dialogue between the Indo-Greek King Menander I (Milinda) and the Buddhist sage Nagasena. It uses clear analogies, such as a flame transferring from one candle to another, to explain complex concepts like rebirth without a soul and the nature of *nirvana*.

THE BARDO THÖDOL (Tibetan Book of the Dead): A guide for the consciousness in the intermediate state (*bardo*) between death and rebirth. It describes the dissolution of the elements at death and the encounter with peaceful and wrathful deities, aiming to help the deceased recognise the clear light of reality and attain liberation.

Jainism

Tattvartha Sutra: A foundational text of Jain philosophy written by Umaswati. It systematises Jain doctrine, detailing the nature of the soul (*jīva*), the influx of karmic matter, and the cosmology of the universe as a "Cosmic Man" (*Loka-Purusha*), offering a rigorous framework for understanding spiritual liberation.

Ancient Egypt

The Book of the Dead (Book of Going Forth by Day): A collection of spells and instructions placed in tombs to help the deceased navigate the afterlife (*Duat*). It famously depicts the "Weighing of the Heart" ceremony, where the deceased's heart is weighed against the feather of *Maʿat* (truth and justice) to determine their fate.

Greco-Roman Philosophy

Plato's Republic (The Myth of Er): The concluding story of Plato's *Republic*, which recounts a soldier's journey to the afterlife. It describes a system of judgment and the "Spindle of Necessity," where souls choose their next lives before drinking from the *River Lethe* to forget their past, emphasising moral responsibility and rational choice.

Virgil's Aeneid (Book VI): The Roman epic poem that follows the hero Aeneas into the underworld to meet his father. It vividly describes the geography of the afterlife, including the *Fields of Elysium* and the *River Lethe*, blending mythology with philosophical ideas about the soul's purification and return.

Plotinus' The Enneads: The collected writings of the founder of Neoplatonism. Plotinus describes the soul's emanation from the "ONE" and its descent into matter, framing life as a journey of purification to return to the divine source, influencing centuries of Western mystical thought.

Christianity

Dante Alighieri's The Divine Comedy: An epic poem that synthesises medieval Christian theology with classical philosophy. It maps the soul's journey through three realms: *Inferno* (Hell), *Purgatorio* (Purgatory), and *Paradiso* (Heaven), creating a structured moral geography of sin, purification, and divine union.

JUDAISM (KABBALAH)

SHA'AR HAGILGULIM (GATE OF REINCARNATIONS): Based on the teachings of the mystic Isaac Luria (the Arizal) and recorded by his disciple Chaim Vital. This key Kabbalistic text explains the concept of *gilgul* (reincarnation), detailing how souls return to rectify past actions (*tikkun*) and fulfils specific spiritual missions.

ISLAM (SUFISM)

RUMI'S MATHNAWI: A massive collection of poetry by the 13th-century Persian mystic Jalaluddin Rumi. Often called the "Quran in Persian," it uses stories and metaphors to explore the soul's evolutionary journey from mineral to plant to animal to human, seeking reunion with the Divine Beloved.

INDIGENOUS TRADITIONS (WEST AFRICA)

IFÁ LITERARY CORPUS: The vast oral tradition of the Yoruba people, preserved by priests (*Babalawo*). It contains verses and stories that explain the concepts of destiny (*Ori*), character (*Ìwà*), and ancestral rebirth (*Atúnwá*), offering a comprehensive worldview of the relationship between the living and the spiritual realms.

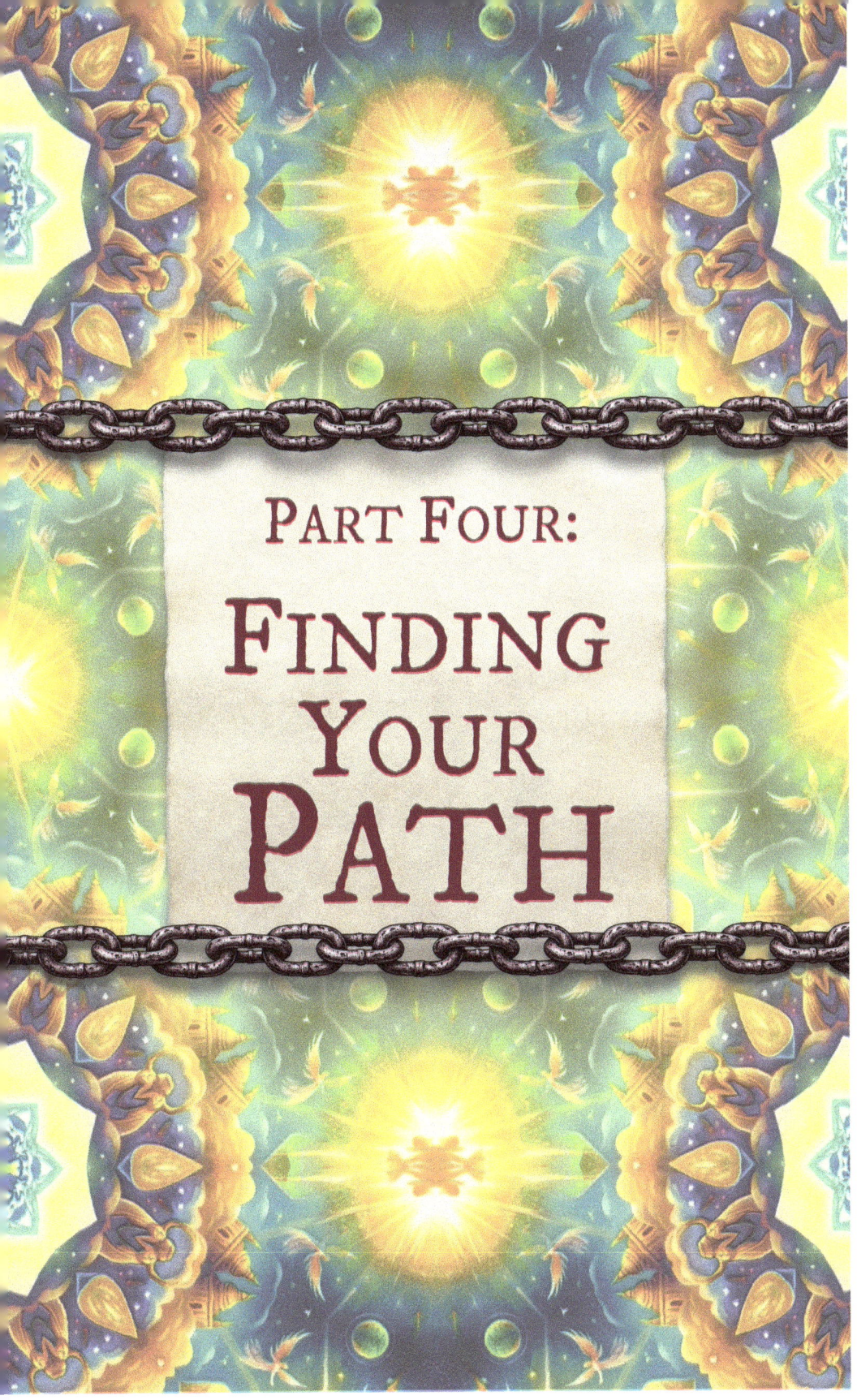

Finding Your Path

BY NOW YOU'VE WALKED THROUGH IDEAS THAT SPAN CONTINENTS and centuries—maps drawn by poets, philosophers, mystics, and scientists. Each offers a different angle on what might unfold beyond a human life, yet all point back to the same place: the unfolding of experience right here. Before turning inward, pause for a moment. Let the dust settle. The next section is not another system to adopt, but a quiet invitation to notice the terrain of your own mind.

We have travelled a long way through the ideas of others—philosophers, physicians, mystics, and entire civilisations—each attempting to describe what happens beyond the final breath. Their cosmologies differ in scale and temperament, yet all share a single observation: human experience does not stop at the edge of the physical body. Something continues, changes, or returns.

But even the most elaborate maps can only take us so far. They show possibilities, not destinations. What matters now is not whether one system is correct, but how these perspectives help us understand our own lives—how we think, how we act, and how we respond to the moments that shape us.

If there is a common thread across every tradition, it is this: the quality of the inner life determines the direction of the outer one. Whether we imagine a wheel, a ladder, or a lineage, all agree that our choices leave impressions. Our habits of mind become the terrain we walk on.

This is where we turn inward. Part Four is not another map of the unseen; it is an invitation to recognise the immediate landscape of your own mind—the shifting states, reactions, and tendencies that influence every moment. Understanding these patterns does not require belief, only curiosity. With even a little awareness, life becomes easier to navigate, and the path ahead becomes clearer

We have looked at the maps of the universe. Now, we must look at the compass: your own mind.

THE ROAD AHEAD

FROM MY OWN EXPERIENCE, BOTH AS A CLINICIAN AND AS SOMEONE who has spent a long time watching minds — including my own — the twelve unwholesome cittas described in Buddhist psychology come remarkably close to a distilled "compass" for spiritual orientation. It is hard to imagine any genuine spiritual progress that ignores the consequences of selfish, harmful, or indifferent actions. Whatever language we use — *karma*, ethics, character, conscience — the basic truth is the same: how we relate to others and to our own experience shapes the direction of our lives.

Every authentic path is unique. No one can walk yours for you, and you cannot be pushed or argued into one. Something in you has to be genuinely thirsty for understanding. My own leaning towards Buddhism does not mean it is superior to any other tradition; it simply reflects the fact that, for me, high-quality, systematic teaching has been most easily available in this form. The *Abhidhamma* — the analytical psychology of early Buddhism — offers a very precise description of how the mind behaves, and it is from there that the list of twelve unwholesome cittas comes.

Even here, you are not being asked for blind faith. The Buddha repeatedly discouraged that. In the famous advice to the Kalamas, he warned against accepting teachings just because they are ancient, respected, logical, or taught by someone we admire. Instead, he encouraged people to test things in their own experience: look at what leads to harm and what leads to benefit, and then live accordingly. The teachings are like a raft used to cross a river — once you have crossed, you don't tie the raft to your back and carry it everywhere. Concepts are tools, not possessions. They point beyond themselves.

The twelve cittas are best approached in that spirit. They are not a moral scoreboard. They are a set of carefully observed patterns that can help you see, with more honesty and less drama, what is happening when the mind tightens, contracts, or moves in unhelpful ways.

You do not have to "believe in" them. You simply have to be a little curious.

THE 12 UNWHOLESOME CITTAS
(*Akusalacittāni*)

THESE STATES ARE CLASSIFIED BY THEIR ROOT (GREED, HATRED, Delusion), their FEELING (Joy, Displeasure, Equanimity), their VIEW (Wrong View or lack thereof), and whether they are PROMPTED (induced/hesitant) or UNPROMPTED (spontaneous).

A NOTE ON THE EXAMPLES You will notice that the examples below—a boy stealing an apple, a man in a fit of rage—are drawn directly from ancient commentaries. They may seem simple, perhaps even archaic.

This simplicity is intentional. In our modern lives, our stories are complex and messy. By using simple, stripped-down examples, the Abhidhamma isolates the specific *mental quality* at play (the "flash" of the mind) without getting lost in the details of the story. As you read them, try to substitute "stealing an apple" with your own modern equivalents: sending a passive-aggressive email, doom-scrolling when you know you should sleep, or talking yourself into a purchase you can't afford.

There are eight types. "Greed" here covers all degrees of attraction, from INTENSE PASSION to SUBTLE ATTACHMENT.

THE CORE DISTINCTIONS:

WRONG VIEW (*diṭṭhi*): This does not just mean "having an opinion." It specifically refers to the belief that there are no moral consequences to actions (denying *kamma*) or that harmful actions are actually virtuous.

PROMPTED (*sasaṅkhārika*): The action requires urging, either by others (a friend saying "do it") or by oneself (deliberately talking oneself into it).

UNPROMPTED (*asaṅkhārika*): The action is spontaneous, immediate, and requires no external pressure or internal hesitation.

WHY "PROMPTING" MATTERS

Modern readers often think "Spontaneous" (Unprompted) is "better" or "more innocent" than "Premeditated" (Prompted). In Buddhism, it's often the opposite—spontaneous greed implies a habit is so deep you don't even hesitate.

We often assume that a premeditated act is "worse" than a spontaneous one. But in the architecture of the mind, Unprompted (spontaneous) states reveal our deepest habits.

If you get angry *instantly* (Unprompted), it suggests the root of anger is strong within you. If you get angry only after someone goads you (Prompted), the root is slightly weaker. Watching whether your reactions are prompted or unprompted helps you see how deeply a habit has taken hold.

Table 18. The Twelve Unwholesome Citta
- From Bhikkhu Bodhi's Comprehensive Manual of Abhidhamma

#	Root	Feeling	Associated with	Prompted
1	Greed	Joy	Wrong View	No
2	Greed	Joy	Wrong View	Yes
3	Greed	Joy	No Wrong View	No
4	Greed	Joy	No Wrong View	Yes
5	Greed	Neutral	Wrong View	No
6	Greed	Neutral	Wrong View	Yes
7	Greed	Neutral	No Wrong View	No
8	Greed	Neutral	No Wrong View	Yes
9	Hatred	Displeasure	Aversion	No
10	Hatred	Displeasure	Aversion	Yes
11	Delusion	Neutral	Doubt	—
12	Delusion	Neutral	Restlessness	—

A. CONSCIOUSNESS ROOTED IN GREED
(*Lobha-mūla-cittāni*)

1. GREED + WRONG VIEW + UNPROMPTED + JOY

EXPLANATION: You DESIRE an object or act and seize it SPONTANEOUSLY with a HAPPY heart, while holding the SPECIFIC VIEW that there is no evil or karmic consequence in doing so.

ABHIDHAMMA EXAMPLE: With joy, holding the view that there is no evil in stealing, a boy spontaneously steals an apple from a fruit stall.

2. GREED + WRONG VIEW + PROMPTED + JOY

EXPLANATION: Similar to the above (joyful and believing there is no moral fault), but the desire is SLUGGISH or HESITANT. It arises only after someone else URGES you, or after you DEBATE WITH YOURSELF to build up the motivation.

ABHIDHAMMA EXAMPLE: With joy, holding the same view (that there is no evil in it), a boy steals an apple through the prompting of a friend.

3. Greed Unprompted+Joy

EXPLANATION:	You engage in a greedy act spontaneously and happily, but YOU *KNOW* IT IS WRONG. You possess the "Right View" that this action is unwholesome, but your desire is SO STRONG that you do it anyway, without hesitation.
ABHIDHAMMA EXAMPLE:	(Same as #1, but the boy does *not* hold any wrong view). He knows stealing is wrong, yet sees the apple and spontaneously grabs it with joy.

4. Greed Prompted +Joy

EXPLANATION:	You KNOW the act is WRONG. You feel some hesitation or lack of energy initially, but after ENCOURAGEMENT (from a friend or your own internal rationalisation), you engage in the act with enjoyment.
ABHIDHAMMA EXAMPLE:	He knows stealing is wrong. A friend urges him to do it. After this prompting, he steals the apple with joy.

5. Greed+Wrong View+Unprompted +Equanimity

Explanation: The act is SPONTANEOUS and you believe there is NO KARMIC CONSEQUENCE (Wrong View), but there is no intense joy. The feeling is neutral (*upekkhā*). This often happens when the pleasure is mild or the act has become a routine habit.

Abhidhamma Example: A boy spontaneously steals an apple believing there is no sin, but does so with a neutral feeling (perhaps he is not hungry, or simply habituated to stealing).

6. Greed+Wrong View+Prompted +Equanimity

Explanation: You believe the act has NO MORAL CONSEQUENCE, but you need PRODDING to do it. When you finally act, you feel neither pleasure nor displeasure, just neutrality.

Abhidhamma Example: Induced by a friend, believing there is no sin, he steals with a neutral feeling.

7. GREED UNPROMPTED+EQUANIMITY

EXPLANATION:	You KNOW the act is WRONG. You do it SPONTANEOUSLY (without hesitation), but WITHOUT ANY EXCITEMENT OR JOY. It is a dry, passive attachment.
ABHIDHAMMA EXAMPLE:	Knowing it is wrong, he spontaneously steals the apple but feels nothing in particular (neutral feeling).

8. GREED PROMPTED+EQUANIMITY

EXPLANATION:	You KNOW the act is WRONG. You are hesitant or sluggish. After being URGED, you do it, but without enjoyment.
ABHIDHAMMA EXAMPLE:	Knowing it is wrong, and only after being pressured by a friend, he steals the apple with a neutral feeling.

B. CONSCIOUSNESS ROOTED IN HATRED
(Dosa-mūla-cittāni)

There are two types. These are the only consciousnesses accompanied by DISPLEASURE (*domanassa*) and AVERSION (*paṭigha*). KEY NOTE: Hatred *never* coexists with joy, and it is never associated with "Wrong View" in the same immediate moment (though Wrong View might motivate it previously).

9. HATRED+AVERSION+UNPROMPTED+DISPLEASURE

EXPLANATION:	A SPONTANEOUS flare-up of ANGER, RAGE, or ILL-WILL. It arises IMMEDIATELY without any prior planning or encouragement.
ABHIDHAMMA EXAMPLE:	With hatred, a man murders another in a spontaneous fit of rage.

10. HATRED+AVERSION+PROMPTED+DISPLEASURE

EXPLANATION:	This is anger that is "worked up." It could be PREMEDITATED malice (planning revenge) or ANGER that arises after listening to someone else's inflammatory words. It is sluggish or induced rather than instantaneous.
ABHIDHAMMA EXAMPLE:	With hatred, a man murders another after premeditation (planning) or encouragement.

C. CONSCIOUSNESS ROOTED IN DELUSION
(*Moha-mūla-cittāni*)

There are two types. Delusion is present in ALL UNWHOLESOME STATES, but in these two, it is the DOMINANT ROOT, standing alone without Greed or Hatred. KEY NOTE: These are always accompanied by EQUANIMITY (neutral feeling). They are confused, not happy or sad.

11. DELUSION+DOUBT (*Vicikicchā*)

EXPLANATION:	This is not merely "intellectual questioning" but a SPIRITUAL PARALYSIS. It is a wavering, perplexed state where one cannot decide or gain confidence in the truth. Specifically, it refers to doubting the Enlightenment of the Buddha, the efficacy of the *Dharma* (teaching), or the law of *karma*.
ABHIDHAMMA EXAMPLE:	A person, due to delusion, doubts the enlightenment of the Buddha or the efficacy of the *Dhamma* as a way to deliverance.

12. DELUSION+RESTLESSNESS (*UDDHACCA*)

EXPLANATION:	This is "distraction" or "agitation." The mind is SCATTERED and cannot stay fixed on a single object. Unlike the other cittas, restlessness is a factor in *all* unwholesome states, but here it is the *chief* factor. It is the "pure" state of being scattered.

You, Again

ABHIDHAMMA EXAMPLE: A person is so distracted in mind that he cannot focus his mind on any object.

NOTE REGARDING PROMPTING FOR DELUSION: The Abhidhamma manuals generally classify these two delusion cittas as Unprompted because they occur naturally without needing inducement, though there is some commentary debate on this)

If you're curious to explore the Abhidhamma in more depth—particularly how these cittas fit into the wider architecture of Buddhist psychology—a beautifully structured starting point is A Comprehensive Manual of Abhidhamma by Bhikkhu Bodhi. It offers a clear, systematic overview without assuming prior knowledge. For an accessible introduction through spoken teaching, I also recommend searching YouTube for Bhikkhu Bodhi's lectures on the Abhidhamma; his explanations are careful, grounded, and wonderfully steadying. You don't need this background to work with the cittas, but if you enjoy understanding the deeper framework, these resources are the most reliable guides.

How to Work With This List

THE CITTAS ARE NOT THERE TO MAKE YOU FEEL JUDGED. THEY ARE there to help you recognise, with more clarity and less self-attack, how your mind moves.

Simply naming a state — "this is greed," "this is irritation," "this is restlessness" — already changes your relationship with it. It shifts you from being completely inside the experience to having a small vantage point from which to observe it.

Over time, you may begin to notice that each unwholesome citta has a natural medicine: generosity softens greed, kindness cools hatred, and clear seeing dissolves delusion. You don't have to force this. Just noticing that these opposites exist is often enough to let them arise more easily.

Throughout all of this, gentleness is essential. The aim is not to condemn yourself for having unwholesome moments. The aim is to become familiar with them, so that you are less compelled by them and less certain that "this is who I am." Even the darkest citta can become a teacher if it is met with honesty and kindness.

Nigredo

As you become more familiar with these inner movements, you may notice that certain layers of experience start to loosen. The world might feel slightly less solid. Old assumptions soften. Some days there may be uncertainty or restlessness — not as a dramatic crisis, but as a gentle melting of structures that once felt permanent.

Alchemy called the beginning of this soft collapse *nigredo* — the darkening. Not darkness, not catastrophe; simply the recognition that the familiar is losing its fixed shape, and that something more truthful may be emerging underneath.

You do not need to go looking for this. If it becomes relevant in your life, you will recognise it. If you ever feel drawn to walk more deliberately into that territory, the longer work of *Nigredo* is there as a companion, but it is not a requirement, and it is certainly not a badge of seriousness.

For now, it is enough to treat these cittas as a kind of weather map for the mind. Noticing them steadily, without drama and without harshness, already reduces confusion and brings a little more space into each day.

CLOSING THOUGHTS

Your path will unfold according to your temperament, your challenges, your insights, and the conditions of your life.

There is no need to force progress or manufacture certainty.

If you understand these twelve cittas—even lightly—you already have a dependable framework for recognising the mind's habits. And once you can recognise those habits, you can begin to loosen them.

Everything else grows from that.

If you ever feel the pull to explore deeper stages of inner transformation, especially those described in the alchemical traditions, then *Nigredo* is the natural next step.

But for now, it is enough simply to observe your mind gently, honestly, and with a little more understanding than you had yesterday.

That alone is *meaningful* progress.

That alone *improves a life*.

Appendix

GLOSSARY

ABOSOM A<small>KAN</small> Lesser deities or spirits serving as intermediaries between humans and the Supreme Being, *Nyame*.

AKH A<small>NCIENT</small> E<small>GYPT</small> The transfigured, luminous spirit formed by the union of *Ba* and *Ka*, surviving death as an eternal, effective being.

AKUSALA CITTA B<small>UDDHISM</small> Unwholesome consciousness. Any mind-moment rooted in greed, hatred, or delusion, generating suffering and perpetuating rebirth.

ANAMNESIS G<small>REEK</small> Recollection or un-forgetting. Plato's idea that learning is the soul remembering truths known before birth.

ANATTĀ B<small>UDDHISM</small> No-self. The doctrine that no permanent, unchanging soul exists —only a dynamic stream of processes.

ĀTMAN H<small>INDUISM</small> The eternal Self, identical in essence to Brahman, the ground of all reality.

ATÚNWÁ Y<small>ORUBA</small> Ancestral return. The belief that ancestors are reborn within their lineage to complete or continue their destiny.

AYANMÓ Y<small>ORUBA</small> A person's fundamental, divinely bestowed life-path or destiny.

AYENMO / AYANMO Y<small>ORUBA</small> Variant form of *Ayanmó*; the pre-chosen pattern of one's earthly life.

BA A<small>NCIENT</small> E<small>GYPT</small> The personality-soul—mobile and free to travel between the tomb and the living world.

BARDO T<small>IBETAN</small> B<small>UDDHISM</small> The intermediate state between death and rebirth, marked by visionary and psychological experiences shaped by karma.

BAQĀ' S<small>UFISM</small> Subsistence. The enduring pstate of abiding in G<small>OD</small> that follows the annihilation of ego (*fanā'*).

BRAHMAN H<small>INDUISM</small> The absolute, unconditioned reality underlying all phenomena; the infinite ground of being.

CITTA P<small>ĀLI</small>/S<small>ANSKRIT</small> Mind or consciousness. In Buddhist psychology, the smallest unit of awareness—a mind-moment.

CITTA-SANTĀNA B<small>UDDHISM</small> The stream of mind. The continuous flow of momentary consciousness that gives the illusion of a stable self.

CUTI-CITTA B<small>UDDHISM</small> The death-consciousness, the final mind-moment in a given life.

DAO D<small>AOISM</small> The Way. The ineffable source, pattern, and natural order of the cosmos.

DHARMA / DHAMMA
—In Hinduism, duty, cosmic law, or moral order.

—In Buddhism, the Buddha's teachings and the true nature of reality.

DHARMAKĀYA M<small>AHAYANA</small> B<small>UDDHISM</small> The truth body of the Buddha — the formless, ultimate reality.

DIYU C<small>HINESE</small> C<small>OSMOLOGY</small> The layered underworld through which the dead travel for purification and karmic resolution.

EKPYROSIS S<small>TOIC</small> / N<small>EOPLATONIC</small> A cosmic conflagration through which the universe is cyclically dissolved and reborn.

EIN SOF K<small>ABBALAH</small> The infinite, unknowable aspect of G<small>OD</small>, beyond all attributes.

FANĀ' S<small>UFISM</small> Annihilation. The dissolving of ego in the experience of divine presence.

GATI BUDDHISM The realms of rebirth — heavenly, human, animal, ghostly, and hellish — conditioned by karma.

GILGUL NESHAMOT KABBALAH The rolling or transmigration of souls through multiple lives for rectification.

HARAE SHINTŌ Ritual purification that removes impurity (kegare) and restores harmony.

HEL NORSE The underworld realm of the dead; also its ruler.

HUA DAOISM Transformation; the process by which all things continuously change and cycle.

HUN AND PO CHINESE DUAL SOULS:

HUN — the yang, ethereal soul that ascends.

PO — the yin, earthly soul that remains with the body.

IK ONKAR SIKHISM One Supreme Reality. The foundational concept of Sikh metaphysics.

JĪVA HINDUISM/JAINISM The individual soul or life-monad subject to karma and rebirth.

KADDISH JUDAISM A prayer recited in mourning, affirming divine sanctity.

KAMI SHINTŌ Spirits, deities, forces of nature, or sacred presences encountered in the world.

KAMMA / KARMA BUDDHISM/HINDUISM Intentional action that generates consequences shaping future experience and rebirth.

KARMIC MATTER JAINISM Subtle particles that cling to the soul due to passion and activity, weighing it down and determining its rebirth.

KEVALA JAINISM Absolute knowledge attained when karmic matter is fully shed.

KEGARE SHINTŌ Ritual impurity arising from death, disorder, or misfortune.

LUNG TIBETAN BUDDHISM Psychic wind. Subtle energies that move consciousness through the body and the between-states (bardos).

MA'AT ANCIENT EGYPT Cosmic truth, justice, and order; the principle against which a soul's heart is weighed after death.

MAYA / MĀYĀ HINDUISM Illusion; the apparent world of forms that conceals the underlying unity of Brahman.

MOKṢA HINDUISM/JAINISM Liberation from saṃsāra and the end of karmic bondage.

MUJŌ JAPANESE BUDDHISM Impermanence — the transient nature of all conditioned things.

NAFS ISLAM The soul or self, ranging from base impulses (nafs al-ammārah) to the tranquil self (nafs al-muṭma'innah).

NĀRAKA BUDDHISM/HINDUISM Hell realms characterised by intense suffering, usually temporary and shaped by karma.

NESHAMAH JUDAISM The divine soul, higher than the nefesh and ruach.

NIBBĀNA / NIRVĀṆA BUDDHISM Blowing out. The extinction of craving and suffering; ultimate liberation.

NIGREDO ALCHEMY The Blackening. The dissolving or darkening phase where old structures break down, preparing for transformation.

NIYYAH ISLAM Intention — the moral orientation underlying any action.

NKRABEA AKAN One's destiny or life-purpose, carried by the soul (Okra).

NOUS NEOPLATONISM The divine intellect; the first emanation from the One.

OKRA AKAN The life-soul or divine spark that carries destiny (Nkrabea).

ORI / ORÍ Yoruba Literally "head." The inner spiritual essence and destiny chosen before birth.

PAÑÑĀ Buddhism Wisdom, the direct understanding of the true nature of phenomena.

PATISANDHI-CITTA Buddhism The "rebirth-linking" consciousness that arises at conception and connects one life to the next.

RŪPA Buddhism Form or matter; one of the five aggregates that constitute experience.

SAMSĀRA Indian religions The cycle of birth, death, and rebirth driven by *karma* and craving.

SAMSKARA / SAMSKĀRA Indian religions Conditioning forces or mental formations shaping perception and behaviour.

SEFIROT Kabbalah The ten emanations through which divine energy flows into creation.

SEM-GYU Tibetan Buddhism The "mind-continuum" carried through the *bardos*.

SHEOL Hebrew Bible The shadowy abode of the dead.

SHIVAH Judaism Seven-day mourning period following burial.

SHLOSHIM Judaism Thirty-day period of extended mourning.

SIDDHA Jainism A liberated being who has transcended *karma* and rebirth.

SIDDHAŚILĀ Jainism The realm where liberated *siddhas* exist beyond rebirth.

SKANDHAS Buddhism The five aggregates composing a human being: form, sensation, perception, formations, consciousness.

SUNSUM Akan The personality-spirit that survives death and may become an ancestor.

TAṆHĀ Buddhism Craving or thirst — the root of suffering.

TANASUKH Islamic philosophy Transmigration of the soul; metempsychosis.

THEOSIS Christian mysticism Deification — the process of becoming united with God.

TIKKUN OLAM Kabbalah Repair of the world. The spiritual task of healing creation through righteous action.

TORII Shintō A gateway marking the transition into sacred space.

TUATHA DÉ DANANN Irish tradition A supernatural race associated with the Otherworld and ancestral memory.

UPEKKHĀ Buddhism Equanimity; even-minded balance free from craving and aversion.

VIÑÑĀṆA Buddhism Consciousness; the knowing aspect of experience.

WU WEI Daoism Non-action — effortless action aligned with the natural flow of the *Dao*.

YECHIDAH Kabbalah The highest, most unified level of the soul.

YETZIRAH Kabbalah The world of formation through which divine energy shapes reality.

You, again

APPENDIX

INDEX

Ahiṃsā (non-violence): 90, 109, 188
Akan Tradition (Okra, Sunsum, Nkrabea): 148–150, 221–223
Alchemy: 207–208, 248, 268
Ancestors / Ancestor Veneration / Ancestral Return: 141, 145, 149, 161, 217–223
Ancient Egypt (Ba, Ka, Weighing of the Heart): 191–192
Bardo (Tibetan Buddhism): 40, 105, 181–183
Bhagavad Gītā: 90, 98
Blavatsky, Helena: 80
Bodhisattva: 105, 184
Bowie, David: 48
Bruno, Giordano: 22
Buddhism (Theravāda, Mahāyāna, Vajrayāna): 102–106, 177–184
Caesar, Julius (on Druids): 20, 162
Celtic Tradition: 20, 162–163, 213–215
Christianity: 18, 124–127, 199–201
Churchill, Winston: 92
Citta (Mind-moments): 251–259
Dalai Lama (14th): 88
Dante Alighieri (Divine Comedy): 199–201
Daoism (Laozi, Zhuangzi): 4, 134–138, 225–227
Death (mechanics of transition): 146, 175, 192, 223
Edison, Thomas: 56
Ego (role in rebirth): 130, 221
Emerson, Ralph Waldo: 32
Empedocles: 8
Flammarion, Camille: 54
Ford, Henry: 58

Franklin, Benjamin: 26
Gandhi, Mahatma: 90
Gilgul (Kabbalah): 119, 206
Gnosticism: 125
Greed (Lobha): 252–254
Harrison, George: 46
Hinduism (Ātman, Brahman, Vedas): 96–99, 173–176
Huxley, Aldous: 38
Islam (Sufism, Rumi): 128–131, 207–209
Jainism (Karma as matter, Kevala Jnana): 108–110, 185–188
Jung, Carl: 36
Kabbalah (Tikkun, Sparks): 118–121, 203–205
Karma (definitions across traditions): 90, 97, 104, 109, 175
Leary, Timothy: 40
Lessing, Gotthold Ephraim: 24
MacLaine, Shirley: 50
Memory (past-life research): 64, 68, 70, 72
Neoplatonism: 16, 156, 195
Nigredo: 248
Norse Tradition: 160–161
Origen of Alexandria: 18
Pasricha, Satwant K.: 72
Plato (Myth of Er, Phaedo): 10, 155, 197
Plotinus: 16, 156
Pythagoras: 6
Ram Dass: 42
Ramakrishna: 78
Reincarnation (evidence, philosophy): 2–6, 64–72, 145, 173–188

Saṃsāra: 97, 103, 175
Schopenhauer, *Arthur:* 30
Schweitzer, *Albert:* 62
Shintō *(Kami, Pollution/Purity):* 140–143, 229–231
Sikhism *(Guru Nanak, One Light):* 112–116
Stevenson, *Ian:* 64
Sufism: 130, 207–209
Theosophy: 80, 82
Tucker, *Jim B.:* 68
Virgil: 12, 156
Weiss, *Brian:* 66
Wordsworth, *William:* 28
Yeats, *W.B.:* 34
Yogananda, *Paramahansa:* 86
Yoruba Tradition *(Ori, Atúnwá):* 144–147, 217–219
Zhuangzi: 4

ABOUT THE AUTHOR

Simon Robinson spent the first half of his life mapping the physical body. Trained in medicine at the University of Manchester, he built a career spanning anaesthesia and general practice, earning fellowships from the Royal Colleges in London and Australia.

Yet, beneath the structure of professional success, a deeper restlessness stirred. He found that while medicine could treat the vessel, it often stopped short of the passenger within. This search for something beyond the boundaries of conventional truth led him from the wards of hospitals to the study of the human spirit.

Now based in Scarborough, UK, Simon writes to bridge the gap between clinical rigour and intuitive wisdom. He is the founder of *The Way In, The Way Out* and the author of *A Course in Modern Alchemy*. He writes with a simple intention: not to offer dogmatic answers, but to light a lantern for those navigating the dark.

YOU, AGAIN

APPENDIX

CONTINUING THE WORK:
A Note on Alchemy

IN THESE PAGES, WE HAVE LOOKED AT THE MAPS OF THE AFTERLIFE AND the nature of the soul. But a map is different from the walk itself.

For those who feel a pull to move from theory into direct inner work, I have written a companion curriculum titled *A Course in Modern Alchemy*.

The journey begins with *Nigredo*.

In alchemy, *Nigredo* (blackness) is not a state of depression to be avoided, but a necessary "softening" of the ego. It is the phase where old assumptions loosen, familiar patterns stop working, and we are forced to confront the shadow. It is written for anyone who feels unsettled, disoriented, or unsure of what comes next. *Nigredo* is not a textbook. It is a guide to the "dark night"—a companion for the decomposition of the false self so that something true can eventually take its place.

If you are ready to stop looking for answers outside yourself and begin the slow, honest work of observing the mind, *Nigredo* is available as the first step.

You, Again

Appendix

You, Again

www.ingramcontent.com/pod-product-compliance
Lightning Source LLC
Chambersburg PA
CBHW061229070526
44584CB00030B/4044